W9-BMI-464

the
Weekend
Crafter®

Making
Gingerbread
Houses

the Weekend Crafter®

Making Gingerbread Houses

Dozens of Delectable Designs & Ideas

VERONIKA ALICE GUNTER

LARK BOOKS

A Division of Sterling
Publishing Co., Inc.
New York

EDITOR:
VERONIKA ALICE GUNTER

SENIOR EDITOR:
PAIGE GILCHRIST

ART DIRECTOR:
TOM METCALF

PHOTOGRAPHY:
STEVE MANN

ILLUSTRATIONS:
ORRIN LUNDGREN

EDITORIAL ASSISTANCE:
DELORES GOSNELL
JEFF HAMILTON
REBECCA LIM
NATHALIE MORNU

PRODUCTION ASSISTANCE:
SHAREASE CURL

Library of Congress Cataloging-in-Publication Data

Gunter, Veronika Alice.
  Making gingerbread houses : dozens of delectable designs & ideas /
Veronika Alice Gunter.— 1st ed.
    p. cm. — (The weekend crafter)
  ISBN 1-57990-506-4 (Paperback)
  1. Gingerbread houses. I. Title. II. Series.
TX771.G85 2004
745.5—dc22

                                    2003026268

10 9 8 7 6 5 4 3 2 1

First Edition

Published by Lark Books, a division of
Sterling Publishing Co., Inc.
387 Park Avenue South, New York, N.Y. 10016

© 2004, Lark Books

Distributed in Canada by Sterling Publishing,
c/o Canadian Manda Group, One Atlantic Ave., Suite 105
Toronto, Ontario, Canada M6K 3E7

Published by Lark Books, a division of
Sterling Publishing Co., Inc.
387 Park Avenue South, New York, N.Y. 10016

© 2004, Lark Books

Distributed in Canada by Sterling Publishing,
c/o Canadian Manda Group, One Atlantic Ave., Suite 105
Toronto, Ontario, Canada M6K 3E7

Distributed in the U.K. by Guild of Master Craftsman Publications Ltd.
Castle Place, 166 High Street, Lewes, East Sussex, England BN7 1XU
Tel: (+ 44) 1273 477374, Fax: (+ 44) 1273 478606
Email: pubs@thegmcgroup.com, Web: www.gmcpublications.com

Distributed in Australia by Capricorn Link (Australia) Pty Ltd.
P.O. Box 704, Windsor, NSW 2756 Australia

The works represented are the original creations of the contributing artists. All artists retain copyrights on their individual works.

If you have questions or comments about this book, please contact:
Lark Books
67 Broadway
Asheville, NC 28801
(828) 253-0467

Manufactured in China

All rights reserved

ISBN 1-57990-506-4

CONTENTS

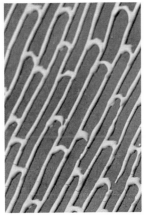

INTRODUCTION

I have to let you in on a secret: With this book and a single weekend, you have everything you need to become a gingerbread house maker. You'll develop skills and ideas that delight, inspire, and amuse. And amaze.

No one will believe that you learned all the tricks of the trade from one book—or that you made your own version of that icon of homemade holiday cheer in just a couple of days.

Thanks to a team of gingerbread experts and talented designers, I was able to put together a how-to book with 17 charming, delectable houses for absolute beginners—who won't feel like beginners for long.

The designs include fresh takes on traditional styles and playful nontraditional themes. The first 11 houses are made from one simple template; variations in doors, windows, and decorating themes make each unique. One house is so easy to make that it doesn't require a template at all. The final five houses are a bit more elaborate, yet they require only minor modifications to the basic template, such as using a new piece or converting a chimney into castle towers.

Whether you want a cottage, cabin, two-story Victorian, or a fabled farmhouse that's not in Kansas anymore, this is the book for you. All of the projects can be done in a weekend, but you can take more time to embellish them, if you like.

The 14 designers of these projects include professional bakers, visual artists, and winners of the annual National Gingerbread House Competition at The Grove Park Inn Resort & Spa in Asheville, North Carolina. They got excited about getting back to the basics of what makes gingerbread houses fun—playing with food, and finishing the project so you can show it off before the holidays pass.

You don't need to have a lot of time on your hands to make a gingerbread house, but you will use your hands—a lot. There's rolling out the dough. Testing its consistency between your fingers. Squeezing icing from a full pastry bag. All of the ingredients used in these houses are edible, so that means you'll also be sculpting soft candies into shapes, arranging beans and grains as sleek details, sorting coarse crackers and pretzels for rustic siding, and cutting sticky gum sticks for window molding.

Pastry chef Aaron Morgan guides you step-by-carefully-photographed step through every detail of Gingerbread Basics—from mixing the dough to putting the finishing touches on your house. You'll also learn dozens of decorating ideas and techniques, and play with special decorating supplies, including chocolate rocks and sugar figurines. In the projects section you'll see complete instructions, how-to photos, illustrations, and tips from the gingerbread house makers. Aaron helped test the engineering of the structures, so you can be sure that your house will not only look good, it will stand tall.

Turn the page and let's make a gingerbread house. Did you say it's your first? I won't tell if you don't.

GINGERBREAD BASICS

Are you ready to a craft a gingerbread house from scratch? Get a taste for baking, building, and decorating with the practical, hands-on lessons in this chapter. Soon you'll be saying *Bring on the dough, icing, and chocolate sprinkles— what I can't sculpt, I'll eat.*

Chances are, you'll enjoy the experience most if you can spread it out over two days. Here's a rough schedule.

S C H E D U L E

• Allow 30 minutes for mixing your dough, plus at least three hours more to refrigerate it. (The colder the dough is, the easier it will be to roll and cut.)

• Plan two hours for rolling, cutting, and baking the dough, and another four hours for letting it cool.

• Budget about an hour and a half for assembling your house, including time for it to dry and settle between stages.

Each house in this book requires only a few hours (or less) of decorating time. Even our five more elaborate houses, beginning on page 58, can be decorated in an afternoon. Of course, you can take any gingerbread house to the next level by adding unique decorative details. The techniques in this book lay the foundation for your future gingerbread house adventures.

Most of the gingerbread house designers featured in this book came up with their best creations using little more than what they found in their kitchen cupboards. We'll cover those common items and other basic decorating supplies in this chapter. But since every well-designed house relies on a solid structure, we'll begin with the basic house design and construction.

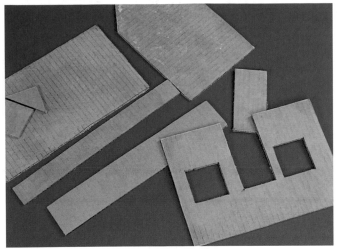
Gingerbread house pattern pieces

Creating Your Pattern Pieces

WHAT YOU NEED

The house template of your choice

Pencil

Pen

Ruler or straightedge

Graph paper (optional)

Cardboard or other sturdy material
(such as poster board or file folders)

Tape

This book features 17 gingerbread house designs. Eleven of them use one basic template, with some slight adaptations or additions to make each house unique. One house is so simple to make that it requires no template. The five more elaborate structures build on the basic template or use a different (but doable) template.

The templates begin on page 76, and each project tells you which ones to use for that house. For example, the Country Chapel uses the Basic House templates, plus the Steeple Base template. It's also easy to adapt the templates if you've got something different in mind but want a starting point.

The basic house template includes four walls and a two-piece roof. There are also templates for adding a porch, a chimney, or a dormer, if you like. These pieces create a structure that is 6 x 10 inches (15.2 x 25.4 cm) at the base and stands 11 inches (27.9 cm) tall from the bottom of the porch to the peak of the roof.

To create your pattern pieces, simply mark the template measurements onto cardboard or any other stiff material, and cut them out. If you're adapting the templates, you may want to measure your pieces on graph paper first, then create them on a stiffer paper. Then—and this step is important—construct your house out of cardboard and masking tape before you even think about dough and icing. We considered repeating that sentence to give it the emphasis it deserves, but decided you might think it was a printing error. Instead, we offer this: When you're up to your elbows in icing trying to fit a fussy chimney piece into place, it will be comforting to draw on the memory that your pattern does fit together the way it's supposed to.

Rolling Out the Dough

WHAT YOU NEED

Flat surface

Rolling pin

Flour

Baking-grade parchment paper (you can use aluminum
foil as a substitute)

Sifter (optional)

Gingerbread dough (page 24)

A baking board is ideal, but any clean flat surface will do for rolling out your dough. Cover your surface with parchment paper and sprinkle flour on the area where you'll roll out the dough. (The dough needs to be able to spread evenly without sticking. You can always brush away excess flour.) Place a portion of dough on top of the floured parchment paper, and begin rolling out the dough with a floured rolling pin. Roll out a portion large enough for a couple of pattern pieces at a time.

PHOTO 1 Use plenty of flour as you roll out your dough.

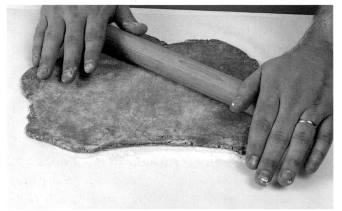

PHOTO 2 Roll gingerbread slightly larger than the pattern pieces.

PHOTO 3 Roll dough to ½ inch (1.3 cm) thick for main supporting walls.

Three things to keep in mind:

1. You don't want the dough to stick to the rolling pin, so sift or sprinkle flour onto the dough before you begin rolling (photo 1).

2. You want the dough piece you're rolling out to be as square and even as possible—and slightly larger than the pattern pieces you plan to cut from it (photo 2).

3. Your rolled-out dough should be approximately ½ inch (1.3 cm) thick if your goal is stability (photo 3). For accent pieces (not the main supporting walls of your house), you can roll the dough a bit thinner if you want a more delicate look.

A floured pizza wheel works best on larger pieces.

Cutting Out Your House

WHAT YOU NEED

Flour

Gingerbread house pattern pieces

Pizza wheel

Small paring knife

Pastry brush

Airtight container for excess dough

Because windows, doors, and other details are essential to the overall look of your gingerbread house, instructions for each project tell you about special cuts you need to make or details you need to add before baking your dough. Be sure to read the instructions before cutting out your gingerbread house pieces.

Begin by lightly dusting the surface of your dough with flour to prevent the pattern pieces from sticking. Then, place as many pattern pieces as will fit on your rolled-out dough and, using the patterns as a guide, begin cutting your dough pieces. A floured pizza wheel works best on larger pieces, since knives can drag and misshape the dough. A small paring knife is perfect for smaller pieces and more intricate cuts, such as those on the chimney. Peel away your excess dough, save it in an airtight container, and refrigerate it. You might use it to make decorations, or to satisfy your appetite when your baked gingerbread house pieces begin to smell irresistible.

Decorating Details

You can score or texturize pieces of unbaked dough so they resemble bricks, wooden planks, or other building materials. You can also texturize pieces of baked gingerbread; this works best on small areas, such as those shown in Pueblo Perfect on page 35 and the Cozy Cabin on page 27. To make colored pieces, you can brush liquid food color, watered-down gel color, or food color paste mixed with water on the dough before baking it.

Texturize gingerbread for a wood plank effect, as shown on this door.

Transferring and Baking Your House Pieces

WHAT YOU NEED

Scissors

Flat cookie sheets

Cut the parchment paper around your individual house pieces, and transfer them—paper and all—to flat cookie sheets. Space your pieces so they're about an inch (2.5 cm) apart, trying to keep larger pieces and smaller pieces on separate trays, since they may finish baking at different times. Use a pastry brush to remove excess flour from the gingerbread, so it doesn't cake during baking.

Bake the gingerbread in an oven preheated to 350°F (177°C) until the dough is deep brown but not black (approximately 20 minutes). If you decide your pieces aren't quite done after they've cooled, stick them back in the oven for a few minutes. Be sure to bake your dough until it's completely dry and crisp—it's a building material, not a cookie.

Remove the cookie sheets from the oven, and allow the pieces to cool for approximately 25 minutes before transferring them to a flat countertop or board. If the surface is uneven, it could cause the pieces to crack or break. Allow the pieces to cool for four hours minimum (overnight if possible) before beginning to assemble your house.

We recommend cutting your house pieces before you bake them (rather than baking a flat sheet of dough and cutting the pieces out of the warm, baked gingerbread). But you can do some quick nips and tucks to the just-from-the-oven gingerbread. Place your patterns back on top of the warm pieces to see if the dough expanded while baking, and trim them back into shape if necessary. You could also save some of the intricate cuts, such as windows and doors, for this stage.

Tools for assembling your house

Assembling Your House

So how do you fabricate these carefully measured and cut pieces into a house that remains standing when you (breathlessly) pull your hands away? By using royal icing, royal icing, and more royal icing.

WHAT YOU NEED

Base

Pencil

Baked house pieces

Royal icing (page 24)

Pastry bag and #7 plain writing tip (plus a damp cloth to keep pastry bag covered when you're not using it)

Serrated knife

Ruler (for evening up some of your pieces, if necessary)

Pastry brush (for dusting away crumbs as you work)

Several temporary braces (Spice jars, cans, or boxes of raisins will do.) (optional)

CHOOSING A BASE

Anything flat or sturdy will work as a base. The basic house will easily fit on a large serving platter, which can be covered with frosting once your house is complete. Or, you might want to purchase a cake board (available at cake decorating shops), or cut out a wooden base and cover it with a decorative material such as gold foil. One-inch-thick (2.5 cm) polystyrene is another good choice for a base, especially if you plan to include lots of freestanding objects (such as candy cane trees) in your landscaping—you can stick them right in the base rather than securing them with icing. For a polished look worthy of a gingerbread house pro, finish the edges of your base by painting them to match the base surface or by covering them with a decorative foil or paper, for example.

BEFORE YOU BEGIN

Review the All the Trimmings section (beginning on page 17) and the instructions for the specific house you have in mind (pages 25 through 75) before you start assembling your house. Some of the decorating techniques, such as attaching heavy candies or tiny, light grains, are easiest if you work with pieces of gingerbread that are lying flat rather than those that are part of the assembled house.

BUILDING

1. Begin by lightly marking in pencil where you want the house to sit on the base. Don't forget the porch or chimney if you're adding either, or any other additional pieces of your structure. Your pattern pieces can help you establish positions.

2. Start with the back and one peaked end piece of your house. Pipe royal icing along the bottom edges, and then place them over the pencil marks you made for them, forming a corner. Pipe additional icing on the inside bottom edges, where your house pieces meet the base (photo 4). Hold them in place for several seconds, until the icing begins to harden. You can also prop them in place with some temporary braces, though chances are the icing will set up so quickly this won't be necessary.

3. Pipe icing along the side and bottom of one of your peaked end pieces (photo 5), and press it in place, gently holding the joints until the piece is secure. Continue building until your four wall pieces are in place (photo 6). Since icing is the glue that holds your house together, be sure to pipe a liberal amount everywhere gingerbread meets gingerbread, then go back over some of the edges, especially on the inside base of your house, for reinforcement.

4. If you are adding a porch, you'll want to attach it now, before attaching the roof. Begin by placing the porch sides, followed by the porch front, and then the porch floor (photos 7 through 9). Let your house dry for 30 minutes minimum before adding the roof or any other structures, such as a porch overhang, chimney, or dormer.

PHOTO 4 Pipe additional icing on the inside bottom edges, where your house pieces meet the base.

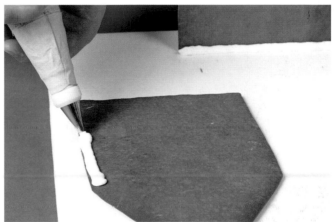

PHOTO 5 Pipe icing along the side and bottom of one of your side pieces.

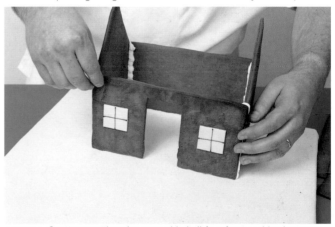

PHOTO 6 Continue until you've assembled all four front and back pieces.

PHOTO 7 Attach the porch sides.

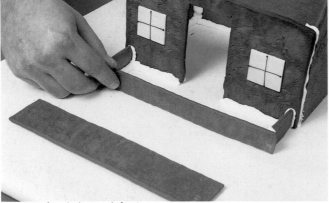

PHOTO 8 Attach the porch front.

PHOTO 9 Attach the porch floor.

PHOTO 10 Position your porch supports and overhang before icing them in place.

PHOTO 11 Set the porch overhang in place.

5. If you are attaching a porch overhang, begin by positioning your porch supports, such as gingerbread columns or candy posts (photo 10). If you have to shave some length off your porch supports, use a serrated knife on the gingerbread columns or a heated knife on the candy canes. You may want to insert the supports temporarily (to help the overhang settle into place), remove them when you decorate the front of your house, then put them back in permanently, and secure them with icing. Pipe icing along the edge of the porch overhang that will attach to the house, and then set it in place (photo 11).

6. Once the porch structure is in place, you can attach the front roof piece. Pipe icing along the top edge of the front house piece, and then attach the front of the roof. It will rest on top of the porch overhang, if you are using one. You may also need to shave your roof pieces slightly to ensure a snug fit (photo 12).

7. Attach the back of the roof by piping icing along the slanted edges of the back side (photo 13), then pressing the roof piece on the slants so that the peak is even with the front and back points. If your roof piece needs some support to keep it from sliding as it settles, use a soda bottle or a box of brown sugar.

8. If your house calls for a chimney, attach it next. To fit the chimney on the side of the house, pipe icing along one outer edge of each 1-inch-wide (2.5 cm) side support, and attach them to the house. Fit the tiny piece with an inverted "V" notch over the peak of the roof to form the fourth side of the chimney, securing it with icing (photo 14). Pipe icing along the outer edges of the

PHOTO 12 Shave the front roof piece, if necessary, before attaching it.

PHOTO 13 Pipe icing for the back roof piece.

PHOTO 14 Fit the notched chimney roof piece over the roof lip.

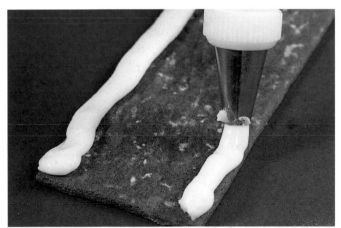
PHOTO 15 Pipe icing along the outer edges of the front chimney wall.

PHOTO 16 Attach the main chimney wall to the side supports.

PHOTO 17 Cover the roof with icing.

PHOTO 18 Add the window dormer.

2-inch-wide (5 cm) front chimney wall (photo 15). Finally, attach the front chimney wall to the side supports (photo 16), holding it in place for a few seconds until the icing begins to harden.

9. If your house calls for window dormers, attach them now. It's easiest to cover the entire roof in a blanket of icing snow (photo 17), and simply position the pieces of the window dormers in the icing. For each dormer, you'll need to attach two triangle pieces to the roof 2 inches (5 cm) apart (the longest side attaches to the roof), and place a square piece on top of them (photo 18).

TIP

If your house pieces are not fitting together evenly, use a serrated knife to straighten up your edges. Be sure to shave the pieces carefully, or more brittle pieces might break. For intricate adjustments, sandpaper or even an emery board will work well. A craft grinder is also a great tool for shaving off pieces of baked gingerbread and whittling down candy canes.

PIPING PRIMER

A 12-inch (30.5 cm) pastry bag is a good size for both building and decorating. Fit your pastry bag with a coupler, which allows you to change tips easily. Attach the decorating tip you want to use, fold the sides of the bag down about one-third of the way, and use a spatula to fill the bag half full with royal icing. Be sure to push the icing down into the tip to avoid air pockets; then twist the end of the bag to seal it. To pipe, apply pressure to the end of the bag and continue twisting it as it empties. Even if you've never used a pastry bag to pipe icing before, you'll easily get the hang of it if you practice on a sheet of wax paper. Do this before you try the same techniques on your house.

TIPS

Working with gingerbread in an especially humid climate? Consider making each exterior wall of your house a double wall by icing two identical pieces of gingerbread together. The icing in between helps draw moisture out of both pieces of gingerbread. In addition, the double walls provide extra support for the roof.

If you're transporting your house to another location, maybe to a competition or so it can serve as a centerpiece at a party or a prize in an auction, assemble everything but the roof and fragile landscaping pieces at home; then attach the roof and finish your decorating on site, if possible.

Making a Paper Piping Cone

For delicate details that require fine piping, you can either use a pastry bag and the tiniest tip you can find, or you can practice some easy kitchen origami and create your own cone. Start with parchment paper, and then follow the steps with photos 19 through 25.

PHOTO 19 Fold the parchment paper to create a triangle.

PHOTO 20 Flatten the edge with a knife.

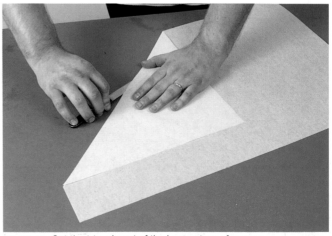

PHOTO 21 Cut the triangle out of the larger piece of paper.

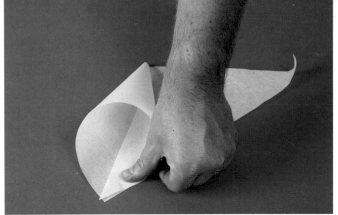

PHOTO 22 Bring one point from the base of the triangle up to the top point.

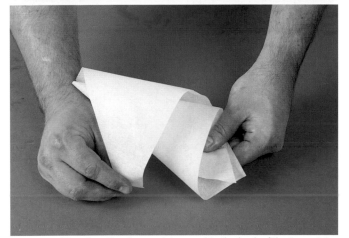

PHOTO 23 Wrap the other base point around to the back of the top point.

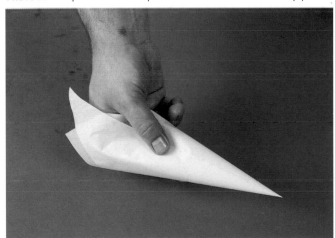

PHOTO 24 Shuffle the paper so that the inside piece is tightening while the outer piece continues to wrap. The action forms a tight grip.

PHOTO 25 Fold in the pieces at the top of the cone to hold the shape in place.

Decorating supplies

All the Trimmings

WHAT YOU NEED

Royal icing (page 24)

Pastry bag and decorating tips (We recommend a #21 star tip, a #16 star tip, a #7 plain tip, a #2 plain tip, and a #352 leaf tip to get started.)

Damp cloth (to keep pastry bag covered when you're not using it)

Small, angled spatula (for spreading icing)

Food color (Food color comes in multiple colors and various forms, including liquid, paste, powder, and gel. Powder is best for coloring chocolates, while paste or gel is ideal for icings.)

Assortment of all things edible (Candy, crackers, cookies, cereal . . . you get the idea. Get familiar with the bulk section of your grocery.)

Wax paper (optional)

Assortment of food colors

Now that you've survived the nerve-wracking part of making gingerbread houses—constructing—you're ready to relax and enjoy the fun part—decorating. Before beginning, make sure you've let your house settle for at least an hour, preferably overnight. Check to make certain it's dry and stable.

So you don't have to improvise while you're still learning to "think gingerbread" on every grocery trip, we've provided lists of What You Need for each project in this book. But don't let that curb your imagination: if you find a way to make copper accents from jellybeans, and prefer them to the plain snack crackers we recommend, go for it. Also, our designers followed tradition and used only edible items to build and decorate the houses in this book. Don't let that stop you from incorporating non-food trinkets, toys, or supports on your house. Use the decorating ideas and techniques below.

ROOF DECOR

The big open space of your roof calls out for imaginative adornment. If you want your roof to look realistic, consider cereal flakes to imitate wood shingles, or shredded wheat squares for a thatched motif. You could also frost your entire roof in white royal icing, simulating a fresh layer of snow.

WINDOWS AND DOORS

Most any sort of wafer cookie or thin candy bar can be used as a propped-open front door or for window shutters. You can also bake your own doors and shutters out of gingerbread, and decorate them with icing and candy.

Sheet Gelatin Windows

Use sheet gelatin to make old-fashioned multi-paned windows, such as the ones on the Storybook Stone Cottage on page 25. Begin by selecting a piece of sheet gelatin larger than the window opening. Working on the inside walls, pipe icing around the opening, approximately ¼ inch (6 mm) from the edge of the opening. Then press a piece of sheet gelatin into the royal icing. Allow the icing to harden before handling the wall. You can buy sheet gelatin in various sizes at cake decorating shops.

Shingling a roof with licorice

A rooftop dusted with shredded coconut snow

Hanging a window made of gingerbread

Sheet gelatin window

Melted Candy Windows

It's easy to make candy windows that look like stained glass. First, cut out your window shapes and begin baking your gingerbread. You must have a piece of parchment paper beneath the gingerbread, or your windows will stick to the cookie sheet. While the gingerbread's baking, use a hammer to crush colored candies in their wrappers (photo 26). Remove the gingerbread piece with window openings from the oven when approximately 5 minutes of baking time remain. Fill the openings with crushed candy, bringing the candy level with the surface of the gingerbread (photos 27 and 28). Stick everything back in the oven for the last 5 minutes of baking. The candy will melt into colored glass windowpanes. Keep a careful watch during the final stage of baking. If left in the oven too long, the melting candy may flow out of the window opening. Allow the candy to cool until it hardens before handling (photo 29).

The colorflow technique creates surfaces with a smooth sheen.

PHOTO 26   PHOTO 27

PHOTO 28   PHOTO 29

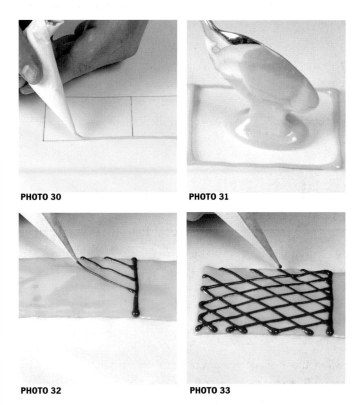

PHOTO 30   PHOTO 31

PHOTO 32   PHOTO 33

COLOR FLOW

For decorative surfaces with a smooth sheen (like the windows and road shown here), use the color flow technique. Begin by creating a thin royal icing by combining a 1-pound box (454 g) of confectioners' sugar, 2 tablespoons of meringue powder, and approximately 3 tablespoons of water. Beat the mixture on a low speed for about 20 minutes, adding more water as you mix if the color flow seems to be too thick. (Beating it on a low speed for a good length of time will help prevent the piped-on color flow from developing air bubbles.) When you've finished mixing, add food color, if you like. With a pencil, draw the pattern you want to create on a piece of wax paper. Pipe your thin icing onto the border of your pattern first (photo 30), using a #3 or #4 decorating tip or a handmade paper cone (the goal here is a thin, fine line), then fill in the interior (photo 31). Let your first color dry thoroughly before adding accents in a new color (photos 32 and 33). Be sure to let your entire creation dry completely (48 hours is recommended), or it will crack immediately when you try to remove it from the paper. Even when they're dry, color flow pieces will be brittle, so handle them with care when you pick them up and ice them into place.

WREATHS AND GARLANDS

With a #352 leaf tip, you can pipe colored royal icing garlands directly onto your porch—or on a fence or gate in the yard. You can also create wreaths by piping circles onto wax or parchment paper. Apply candy decorations before the icing hardens, then let the wreaths dry completely (overnight if you've got the time) before moving them from the paper to their hanging positions on the house. See photos 34 through 36.

PHOTO 34 Making a wreath on a piece of cardboard

PHOTO 35 Pipe pearls of royal icing on the back of the dry wreath.

PHOTO 36 Press the wreath in place until the icing hardens.

PHOTO 41
Different tips create different icing designs for borders and trim.

BOWS

You can make bows from three pieces of a fruit roll up (or fruit leather). Use them to adorn wreaths, doors, and lampposts. Cut two 2-inch-long (5 cm) by ¾-inch-wide (1.9 cm) pieces from the candy (photo 37). Fold each piece into a loop and pinch the ends together (photo 38). Overlap the ends and press them together to make the top section of your bow. Cut a third 2 x ¾-inch (5 x 1.9 cm) fruit roll up piece. Twist and fold middle of the piece, then notch the sides of each end (photo 39). Press the twisted middle of your "ribbon" piece into the top section of the "bow" (photo 40).

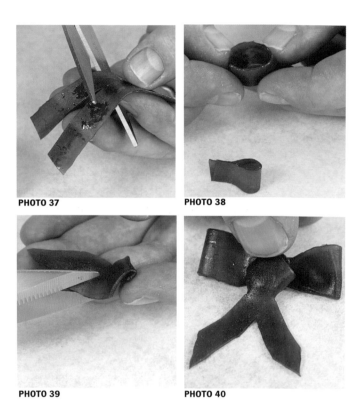

PHOTO 37   **PHOTO 38**

PHOTO 39   **PHOTO 40**

ICING TRIM

Regardless of how you choose to decorate, piping swirls of icing along all the edges, seams, and borders of your house (from doors and windows to the edges of the roof) both provides a finished look and helps reinforce the structure. The icing tips we recommend—attached to a pastry bag—will get you started on a basic variety of decorative borders (photo 41).

These decorations include hot peppers, spices, and marzipan.

BUILDING MATERIALS

Remember when we mentioned learning to "think ginger-bread"? The indoctrination is subtle—it starts with seeing pretzels as 2x4s for ladders and arbors. But, soon enough, it will manifest itself on every aisle of the grocery. You'll identify banana chips as steps, linguine as siding, chocolate kisses as finials, beans as stones, and licorice as molding. You'll know that Tootsie Rolls can be softened in the microwave for a few seconds, and then shaped into everything from stumps to woodpiles. For a sturdy log cabin, you'll recommend attaching rolled-dough logs to the house pieces, and then baking them into place.

Did you know you can create stones that will pass for real rocks by kneading pastillage (page 24) and painting it with food color, wiping away excess color for a marbled effect? Chocolate rocks, chocolate-covered raisins, and walnut pieces work well, too. You won't just be a kid when in a candy store—the bulk section of your supermarket will be your playground.

Herbs create a luscious green lawn.

CREATING ROUNDED STRUCTURES

For rounded shapes such as the structure for Dome Sweet Dome (page 56), rounded bay windows, or any round shape, simply drape pieces of dough over cans (soda and coffee cans are perfect) or pipes, then bake them into shape. First cover the base with aluminum foil or parchment paper. (Masking tape is fine to hold the foil or paper in place. And yes, it will survive the baking process.) Then, grease the foil or paper lightly before adding the dough. You can rest the entire contraption on chopsticks so one side of your rounded structure won't flatten as it bakes.

Rounded structures are easy to make.

LANDSCAPING

You can take care of an afternoon's worth (or, with a little ingenuity, an entire weekend's worth) of digging, planting, mowing, and sprucing—all in the cozy comfort of your kitchen. Landscaping features have almost no limits, and they add loads of character to your gingerbread display.

Dyed and sculpted coconut shavings make hedges to line a path—no pruning required. Spray or lightly soak the coconut in green dye, then use your hands to form the coconut into round or square clumps. For large hedge installations, create a substructure of marshmallows and use royal icing to attach the coconut. Upside-down sugar cones are the perfect shapes for evergreen trees. Cover them with points of green-colored icing (using a #352 leaf tip), and decorate them with candy ornaments such as Red Hots. If you're willing to add inedible pieces to your display, craft stores sell different sizes of polystyrene cones—good to use if you decide to create an entire forest. Or, simplify the process considerably (especially if you're going for a Hansel and Gretel candy cottage look) and stand suckers and lollipops up as instant trees. Sprinkle everything with confectioners' sugar when you're finished, and your entire gingerbread scene will look as if it's just been dusted with snow. For a balmy clime, create a gorgeous green lawn with parsley flakes. Make a skating pond by spreading waves of blue-colored icing on your base or by coloring corn syrup and pouring it into a bordered area. Consider lining your pond with gumdrop rocks or crumbled gingerbread gravel, and toss some sugar crystals on top for chunks of frosty ice. The projects on the pages that follow offer more ideas, including cacti, tumbleweeds, rock gardens, and more.

PASTILLAGE FIGURES

Pastillage is an edible, pliable material similar to stiff putty (photo 42). It is white, but takes color easily. Sometimes referred to as gum paste, pastillage can be sculpted, molded or rolled, cut and shaped. It's long been used to create life-like flowers on top-notch wedding cakes. Flowers, however, are just the tip of the iceberg. Use pastillage for curving architectural structures, drape it in

Pastillage accessories

A napping pastillage elf

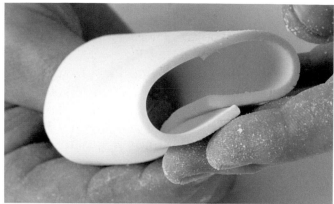
PHOTO 42 Pastillage is pliable.

the form of blankets, or swirl it around a snowman's neck as a scarf. Make a mailbox for the yard, or a newspaper to rest on the porch steps. These details can help bring your holiday creation to life.

Pastillage is easy to work with if you keep a few guidelines in mind. It's important to work quickly, because pastillage dries quickly. It begins to form a crust almost immediately, so keep the bulk of your pastillage wrapped airtight as you work with a little at a time. (We recommend wrapping it in plastic wrap and sealing it in an airtight container.) Pastillage will harden at room temperature in a matter of hours. If it begins to feel tough or is hard to handle, microwave it for a few seconds (literally just two or three seconds) to soften it. Then knead it to a smooth texture to avoid any unwanted cracks or lines in your finished piece.

You can shape pastillage with your hands, or shape it around objects that have a shape you want to achieve, such as a bowl. Just make sure the object is well dusted with powdered sugar, to keep the pastillage from sticking to it. To make animal or human figures, work in sections, then assemble the parts (head, torso, arms, and legs) and attach them to one another by brushing the connections with egg white.

You can also cut out designs from pastillage with kitchen knifes or other cutting tools. Use a file to trim or smooth edges. Whatever you make will harden in minutes into a durable, snow-white decoration, which you can frost, paint with food color, or leave as is.

Best of all, pastillage is a cinch to make; follow the recipe on page 24.

FONDANT FIGURES AND DECORATIONS

A close cousin of pastillage, fondant is in demand for its bright white color and malleability (photo 43). See the striking combination of white and black fondant on the Majestic Mariner's Lighthouse, on page 58. Unlike pastillage, however, fondant contains fat. It will hold its shape (somewhat like soft clay, photo 44), but it will never harden into a rigid form. Premade fondant is available at cake decorating shops (in white and various colors, flavored and unflavored). You can also make your own, using the recipe on page 24.

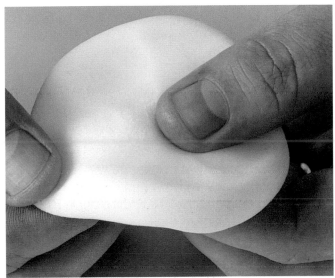

PHOTO 43 Fondant is bright white and malleable.

PHOTO 44 Fondant hold sits shape somewhat like soft clay, but does not become rigid.

MELTED CHOCOLATE FEATURES

There's not much in life that can't be made better with a dose of chocolate. So it goes with gingerbread decor. Melted chocolate, which you can pour, pipe, or dip into, provides just the touch of silky luxury you may be looking for. You can get standard cooking chocolate in wafers and chunks, and in white (which can be colored to match almost any shade) and dark. It's just the thing for dipping and simple piping. To create lattice or something similar, draw the pattern you want to follow, whether it's crisscrosses or elaborate curlicues, on a sheet of white paper. Cover it with see-through wax paper, then pipe according to your design. Freeze the piped chocolate for about an hour, then carefully peel your delicate pieces off the paper and put them in place using royal icing.

If you want to create super-sturdy, stand-alone structures (such as the horse featured in the High Noon Saloon on page 64), you'll have the best results if you use the highest-grade chocolate ("couverture," it's called), and a form. Forms are available at cake decorating shops. To color chocolate, only use oil-based or powdered food colors. (Water-based food colors will ruin the chocolate.)

A white chocolate horse with brown chocolate hooves, hair, and accessories

FINISHING YOUR HOUSE

If you want to preserve your gingerbread house for seasons to come, spray the finished product with a coating of shellac.

Recipes

Use these tried-and-true recipes to make and decorate your gingerbread house. The project instructions that follow this chapter will refer you back to this page.

GINGERBREAD DOUGH

This recipe makes enough dough for the basic house, porch, and chimney illustrated on pages 13 through 15. A heavy-duty mixer will ease the dough-making process. If you don't have one, you're about to learn why bakers are formidable arm wrestlers. (Don't worry, working one batch of dough won't bulk you up.)

CREAM UNTIL LIGHT AND FLUFFY:

2 STICKS (1 CUP OR 230 G) BUTTER (SOFTENED TO ROOM TEMPERATURE)

¾ CUP (100 G) FIRMLY PACKED BROWN SUGAR

ADD AND BLEND ON LOW SPEED:

¾ CUP (250 G) MOLASSES

SIFT, ADD, AND BLEND UNTIL ALL THE FLOUR IS ABSORBED:

5¼ CUPS (630 G) ALL-PURPOSE FLOUR

2 TEASPOONS BAKING SODA

2 TEASPOONS CINNAMON

2 TEASPOONS GROUND GINGER

½ TEASPOON GROUND CLOVES

1 TEASPOON SALT

ADD AND BLEND:

¾ CUP (180 ML COLD WATER)

Spread the dough out on a sheet pan, cover it tightly with plastic wrap, and refrigerate it until you're ready to roll it out (ideally overnight; three hours minimum). It should keep well in the refrigerator for approximately three days.

ROYAL ICING

You should have enough icing to construct and decorate your basic house, plus a porch and chimney, with this recipe. However, because the icing will eventually dry out, you might make just half the recipe for constructing your house, then whip up the second half when you're ready to decorate. (Buying prepared icing won't save you any time or effort—most icing contains shortening or but-ter that will soak into the gingerbread and could cause your house to soften and collapse.)

5¼ CUPS (630 G) CONFECTIONERS' SUGAR

1 TABLESPOON AND 1½ TEASPOONS CREAM OF TARTAR

½ CUP EGG WHITES (120 ML)

Sift the sugar after measuring it. Add the egg whites and cream of tartar to the sugar. Combine the ingredients with a hand mixer on low speed, then beat them on high for two to five minutes, until they're snow-white and fluffy. Keep your icing bowl covered with a damp towel to retain moisture; the mixture crusts quickly when it's exposed to air.

PASTILLAGE (GUM PASTE)

1 TABLESPOON GELATIN

¼ CUP PLUS 2 TABLESPOONS (90 ML) WATER

4½ CUPS (540 G) CONFECTIONERS' SUGAR

Dissolve the gelatin in the water, then add the confec-tioners' sugar and mix well. Keep the mixture covered with a wet towel to prevent it from drying out. The surface may still crust a bit, so sprinkle some more confectioners' sugar in, and knead the pastillage just before using it.

FONDANT

8 TABLESPOONS (1 STICK) UNSALTED BUTTER

¾ TEASPOON VANILLA

¼ TEASPOON SALT

⅔ CUP (225 G) SWEETENED CONDENSED MILK

5 CUPS (600 G) SIFTED CONFECTIONERS' SUGAR

Beat the first three ingredients until they're soft, then add the sweetened condensed milk slowly and beat the mixture until it's very light. Add the confectioners' sugar, cup by cup. Dust your work surface with another cup (120 g) of confectioners' sugar, turn your fondant out onto the surface, and work the sugar into it with your hands. As with pastillage, the surface of your fondant may crust as it sits. If so, sprinkle it with additional confectioners' sugar and knead it just before using it.

Storybook Stone Cottage

This lovely house is fit for an enchanted forest; simple techniques and materials add to the charm.

DESIGNERS: PETE AND SARAH HALL

WHAT YOU NEED

1 batch gingerbread dough (page 24)

1 batch royal icing (page 24)

Cardboard pattern pieces from the Basic House template (page 76)

6 sheets leaf gelatin

1 bag caramels

1 package caramel sticks

1 box shredded wheat cereal

1 Red Hot

Green and red food colors

1 bag shredded coconut

1 bag green decorating sugar

Orange Pixy Stix (or orange decorating sugar)

Gingerbread cutting tools

Pastry bag with tips

Wax paper

Spatula

1 Roll out the dough, and use the cutting tools and cardboard patterns to cut out the house pieces. Cut a large rounded window (2 ¼ x 3 inches [5.7 x 7.6 cm]) in the front wall and the back wall. Cut a medium-sized round window (1 x 2 inches [2.5 x 5 cm]) and a smaller round window (½ inch [1.3 cm] in diameter) in each end wall. Save these cutouts—you'll use them to create the porch steps in step 7. Bake the house pieces, following the instructions on page 11, and allow them to cool.

2 Pipe royal icing on the back side of one window, and attach a sheet of leaf gelatin (photo A). Repeat for each window. Allow the icing to harden.

3 To make the stonework, cut the caramels in three pieces and flatten them on a sheet of wax paper (photo B). Make extra to use on the steps.

4 Apply the flattened caramels to the outside walls with icing (photo C). To create the window box, attach one caramel stick with icing below each window. Allow the icing to harden.

5 Assemble the cottage, following the basic instructions on page 12.

6 Cover the roof with icing. Attach two rows of shredded wheat cereal (photo D). Use icing to attach caramel sticks vertically to the door, and then attach a Red Hot for the doorknob.

7 To make the steps, cut the window cutouts in half. Attach the flattened caramels to the front edges (photo E). Stack them to your desired height, cover them with icing, and attach carmels as shown in the main project photo.

8 Spread icing on the base. Make shrubs from the green food coloring and coconut, following the instructions on page 21. Sprinkle the "lawn" with green decorating sugar, and make the path from orange Pixy Stix sprinkles. Color some icing green, and pipe vines on each side of the door and windows. Use a leaf tip to make leaves for the vines and leaves for the flowers that will go in your window boxes. Pipe pink, yellow, and red flowers, as shown, on the walls, window boxes, and shrubs, using colored icing and a star tip.

A

B

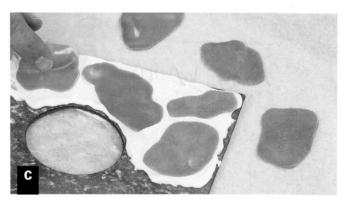

C

D

E

DESIGNER: TODD KINDBERG

Cozy Cabin

Daydream about a holiday retreat in this rustic log cabin, complete with a rocking chair and a handsome chimney.

1 batch gingerbread dough (page 24)

1 batch royal icing (page 24)

Cardboard pattern pieces from the Basic House template (page 76)

Cardboard pattern pieces from the Chimney template (page 76)

Cardboard pattern pieces from the Porch template, minus the Front and Floor sides (page 77)

Assorted hard candies

Green, yellow, and red food colors (optional)

1 bag dry pinto beans

1 bag pretzel rods

Several large pretzel sticks

Several pretzel squares

Several mini pretzels

1 package cinnamon graham crackers

1 bag shredded coconut

1 ice cream cone (called a sugar cone)

1 box powdered sugar

Gingerbread cutting tools

Extra mixing bowl (optional)

Pastry bag with tip

Serrated knife

Spatula

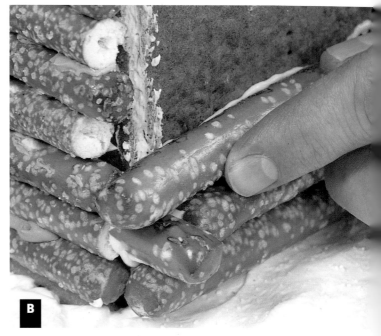

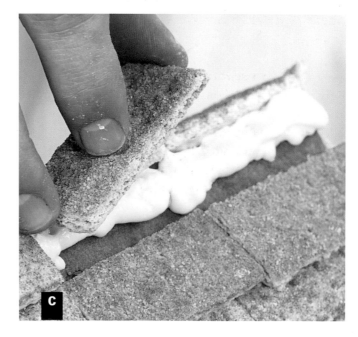

1 Roll out the dough, and use the cutting tools and cardboard patterns to cut out the house pieces. Cut out two 2-inch-square (5cm) windows on the front wall and one 2 x 4-inch (5 x 10.2 cm) door. Save the door—you'll reattach it in step 6. Bake the house pieces, following the instructions on page 11. Five minutes before the pieces are done, make the melted candy windows, following the instructions on page 19. Allow your cabin pieces to cool.

2 Separate one quarter of the royal icing into the extra bowl, and color it greenish-gray (optional). Lay a foundation of pinto beans in colored icing in the area that will be beneath the porch floor. Assemble the cabin using the white icing, following the instructions

on page 12. Use the serrated knife to cut five pretzel rods to fit as the porch overhang supports and as under-the-porch supports, as shown in the main project photo. Use the icing to attach the pretzel rods.

3 Working in sections, spread the colored icing on the chimney and attach the pinto beans (photo A).

4 Begin attaching the pretzel rod logs to the cabin, spreading gray icing on each wall and then pressing the pretzels in place. Stagger the pretzels as you stack them near corners (photo B). When needed, use the serrated knife to cut the pretzel rods to fit. Take half of the remaining white icing and color it gray (optional). Use the pastry bag to pipe gray icing as chinking.

5 Working in sections, cover the roof and porch overhang with the icing of your choice (it won't show), and break the graham crackers into quarters and attach them in rows. Work from the bottom up, and stagger each row (photo C). Create the illusion that the roof was notched to accommodate the chimney by having the shingles overhang on the chimney side, as shown in the main project photo. Cut the crackers into quarters to hang off the roof's edges.

6 Scrape lines into the door to look like boards (photo D). Apply gray icing to the tip of a pretzel stick to create the door handle, and attach it. Use gray icing to attach the door to the house.

7 Make the rocking chair by attaching two pretzel squares to form the back and seat, then attach one mini pretzel to each side, to form the arms (photo E).

8 Cover the base with the white icing, to resemble a snowy yard. Make steps for the porch out of pretzel rod scraps. Make shrubs from the green food color and coconut, following the instructions on page 21. Apply the same concoction to the sugar cone to make a tree. Sprinkle the powdered sugar on the entire scene to resemble a fresh dusting of snow.

D

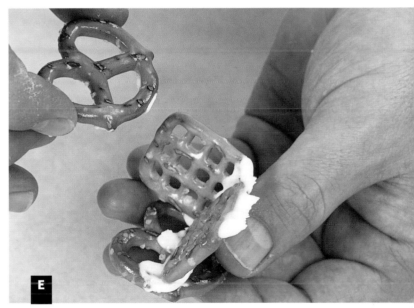
E

DESIGNERS: PETE AND SARAH HALL

Candyland Fantasy

Tempt children of all ages with the colorful collection of candies on this spirited holiday display.

WHAT YOU NEED

1 batch gingerbread dough (page 24)

1 batch royal icing (page 24)

Cardboard pattern pieces from the Basic House template (page 76)

Cardboard pattern piece for the porch overhang from the Porch template (page 77)

1 bag assorted hard candies

1 package candy coconut slices

1 box peppermint sticks

4 pieces black licorice

1 bag gumdrops

10 pieces red licorice lace

10 red licorice twists

2 boxes rainbow jimmies

Green food color

1 bag shredded coconut

Rolling pin (or hammer)

Gingerbread cutting tools

Spatula

Plastic bag

Pastry bag and tips

1 Roll out the dough, and use the cutting tools and cardboard patterns to cut out the house pieces. You won't need the porch sides, floor, or floor front pieces. (You'll use coconut slices instead, in step 4.) Cut two windows in each wall, tracing around a spool and a jam lid to create the different sizes, and one doorway from the front wall. Bake the house pieces, following the instructions on page 11, and allow them to cool.

2 Put the hard candies in the plastic bag. Use the rolling pin to crush the candy (photo A).

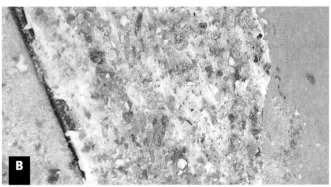

3 Spread icing on each wall, and cover each wall with the crushed candy (photo B).

4 Assemble the house, following the instructions on page 12. Edge each corner of the house with black licorice, cut to length. To build the porch, use the candy coconut slices (cut to length) as the base of the porch floor, attaching them to the base and house with royal icing. Attach the peppermint sticks as porch supports. Attach the porch overhang with icing. Cut more coconut slices and stack them, using icing to create the steps, as shown in the main project photo.

5 Cover the roof with icing. Attach rows of gumdrops. Weave licorice lace between the rows, pushing it into the icing. Edge the roof with red licorice twists (photo C).

6 Use the pastry bag to pipe the window and door edges with icing (photo D).

7 Spread icing on your base. Sprinkle the yard with rainbow jimmies. Build a fence from peppermint sticks and icing (photo E). Make shrubs from the green food color and coconut, following the instructions on page 21 (minus the marshmallows). Use the pastry bag and a star tip to pipe flowers on the shrubs.

DESIGNER: ROSE REITZEL-PERRY

Feathered Friends Houses

For an alternative to a traditional gingerbread house, make a pair of elegant birdhouses with simple designs and natural foods.

WHAT YOU NEED
1 batch gingerbread dough (page 24)
1 batch royal icing (page 24)
Cardboard pattern pieces from the Basic House template (page 76)
Per Birdhouse
4 handfuls wild rice
2 handfuls oat groats
2 handfuls millet
2 handfuls amaranth
4 handfuls pumpkin seeds
4 handfuls poppy seeds
2 handfuls unsalted almonds
1 thick pretzel
2 handfuls French lentils
Gingerbread cutting tools
Wax paper
Spatula
Pastry bag and tips
Serrated knife

BIRDHOUSE 1 *Top project photo*

1 Roll out the dough, and use the cutting tools and cardboard patterns to cut out the house pieces. Cut out one extra end wall. Cut the roof pieces and the two longest wall pieces in half, widthwise. You now have all the parts for two birdhouses. Use a spool as your guide to cut one round doorway in the center of two of the end wall pieces. Bake the birdhouse pieces, following the instructions on page 11, and allow them to cool.

2 Cover your workspace with a sheet of wax paper, and begin work on your first birdhouse. Pour the wild rice onto the paper. Spread royal icing on one side of a roof piece. Dip the roof in the wild rice (photo A). Repeat until the wild rice covers the icing.

3 Lay the roof piece on your workspace, and use the pastry bag to pipe a star of icing atop the wild rice (photo B). Repeat, making three stars, then fill in each star with icing.

33

4 Sprinkle the oat groats on each star (photo C), and edge each with millet grains.

5 Repeat steps 2 through 4 for the second roof piece and for each wall, but this time pipe a tree shape onto each wall, instead of stars. Use sprinkled amaranth to cover the walls, pumpkin seeds to fill in the tree shapes, and poppy seeds to edge each tree.

6 Assemble the birdhouse, following the basic instructions on page 12.

7 Pipe icing along the peak of the roof and the roof edges on each end. Place pumpkin seeds in rows on the edges of the roof (photo D.) Pipe icing along each corner of the house, and attach the almonds.

8 Use the serrated knife to cut the pretzel in half for the perch. Pour out some poppy seeds onto the wax paper, coat the pretzel in icing, and then roll it in the seeds (photo E).

9 Spread icing on the base, and cover it with French lentils. Use icing to attach the pretzel below the doorway (photo F). Prop the pretzel in place with a cup or small vegetable can until the icing hardens.

BIRDHOUSE 2 *Bottom project photo*

Use similar materials, plus dried cranberries, dried corn, and French lentils, to make the second birdhouse. You may want to play with other design motifs, as well. Here, the designer used hearts and diamonds on her second house.

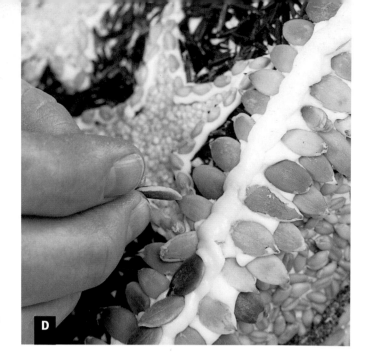

DESIGNER: MEGHAN LUNDY-JONES

Pueblo Perfect

Top adobe color and texture with petite peppers and elegant luminaries for a Southwestern-style home with holiday flair.

1 batch gingerbread dough (page 24)

1 batch royal icing (page 24)

Cardboard pattern pieces from the Basic House template, modified to cut the peak off the end wall pieces, minus the roof pieces (page 76)

Cardboard pattern piece for the Pueblo Roof template (page 76)

1 handful assorted hard candies

Red, yellow, blue, and turquoise food colors

6 pieces of red licorice lace

1 handful red and brown mini M&Ms

4 pretzel rods

6 pretzel sticks

Half a handful chile pequins (tiny red, hot peppers)

2 pumpernickel snack sticks

A pinch of nutmeg or allspice

¼ box brown sugar

1 handful marzipan

½ batch pastillage (page 24) (optional)

2 banana-shaped cookies (found in the baby food section of a grocery store)

1 black food color marker

A pinch of tiny pink or yellow candies

Gingerbread cutting tools

Extra mixing bowl

Chopstick or other carving utensil

Spatula

Paper towels

Pastry bag with tips

1 Roll out the dough, and use the cutting tools and cardboard patterns to cut out the house pieces. Cut two matchbox-sized windows out of the front wall. Cut out one doorway. Bake the house pieces, following the instructions on page 11. Five minutes before the pieces are done, make the melted candy windows, following the instructions on page 19. Allow the pieces to cool.

2 Use the chopstick to scratch the outline of adobe bricks on the surface of a few corners. Scratch the surface of the "bricks" to create a rougher texture. Soften the lines and create an aged adobe appearance by dipping your finger into some water and rubbing the areas you've carved and scratched (photo A). Use the chopstick to outline the shape of the front door.

3 Add red and yellow food colors, plus a touch of blue, to half of the royal icing to give it an adobe hue. Spread this icing onto the walls, avoiding the front door and the areas where you created brick outlines (so it has the appearance of stucco). The icing should be rough in some spots and smooth in others. Create this texture by dipping your finger into some water and floating it over the icing's surface to create smooth spots (photo B). Use paper towels to catch any drips. Allow the icing to harden. Add some turquoise food color to a small quantity of icing thinned with water. Spread it onto the door area. Allow the icing to harden.

4 Assemble your pueblo walls, following the basic instructions on page 12 and using the adobe icing. Then attach the flat roof piece. Make sure it overhangs evenly on each side, as shown in the main project photo.

5 Outline the door and windows with red licorice lace. Using the mini M&Ms, create a knob and decorate the door, as shown in the main project photo.

6 For the arbor, make posts by cutting two pretzel rods to the desired height, and use adobe icing to attach them vertically 3 inches (7.6 cm) in front of the door. Cut two pretzel rods 3 inches (7.6 cm) long, and attach them to the wall so they rest at a right angle on the posts. Lay pretzel sticks across the rods to create the arbor's roof, attaching them with dabs of icing (photo C).

7 Create the chile ristras, or garlands of chile peppers, by dipping chile pequins into adobe icing and sticking them to the front of the arbor post, then to each other as you work upward (photo D). Pipe white icing beneath the arbor, and place mini M&Ms in a pattern to create a tiled stoop, as shown in the main project photo.

8 To create the roof beams, break the pumpernickel snack sticks in half and use adobe icing to attach them, pointing outward and evenly spaced about 1 inch (2.5 cm) apart, to the tops of the front and back walls.

9 Make some tan-colored icing. Apply a thin layer to the base, making sure to spread it right to the sides of the pueblo. To give the ground texture, sprinkle the icing with the nutmeg, allspice, and brown sugar, and blend it with a spatula.

10 Use your choice of icing, pretzel rods, and pretzel sticks to make a ladder. When it's dry, lean it against the roof on the side of the house, and attach it with more icing. Make farolitos, or luminaria, by flattening a small amount of marzipan (or pastillage, page 24) with your fingers, cutting out a rectangle, and shaping it like a bag. Attach luminaria along the roof's edge, under the arbor, and in the yard using the adobe, tan, or white icing.

11 To make the saguaro cactus, color some pastillage green, and apply it to a pretzel rod in very thin layers by pressing it on with your fingers. Use the same technique to apply green pastillage to two banana-shaped cookies. Attach the ends of the cookies to the pretzel with icing, cover the seams with pastillage, and allow the icing to harden. Draw spikes on the cactus with the black food color marker. Attach the cactus to the base with icing. Create a prickly pear cactus by shaping flattened pastillage into four teardrop shapes and joining them. Press tiny pink or yellow candies into place for the flowers. Press the finished prickly pear against the front wall.

A

B

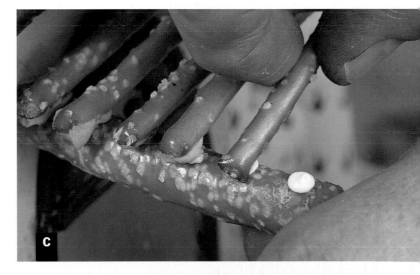

C

D

Bamboo-Roofed Teahouse

Offset the holiday hustle and bustle with the neutral hues and Zen features of a traditional Oriental teahouse.

DESIGNER: DIANA LIGHT

WHAT YOU NEED

1 batch gingerbread dough (page 24)

1 batch royal icing (page 24)

Cardboard pattern pieces from the Basic House template (page 76)

Cardboard pattern pieces from the Teahouse Roof template (page 78)

Beige and brown food colors

12 small pretzel sticks

1 small bag white sugar

1 handful banana chips

2 handfuls roasted, salted sunflower seeds

3 large pretzel sticks

1 handful peanuts

Gingerbread cutting tools

Ruler

Pencil

Paper

Wax paper

Pastry bag and tips

Small angled spatula

Fork

1 Roll out the dough, and use the cutting tools and cardboard patterns to cut out the house pieces. Bake the house pieces, following the instructions on page 11, and allow them to cool.

2 Color all of the royal icing a light brown, then use it to assemble the walls of the house, following the instructions on page 12. (You'll assemble the roof in step 4.)

3 Measure and mark on a piece of paper the sizes and shapes of your doors and window. (This house features two 1 x 2-inch [2.5 x 5 cm] doors and a 5 x 4 ½-inch [12.7 x 11.4 cm] window.) With your marks as guides, use the color flow technique on page 19 to make your doors and window. (Use the brown food color to color the icing for the window grid.) Let them dry. Carefully lift each piece off the wax paper and use icing to attach the window and doors to the walls (photo A). Frame each door with small pretzel sticks.

4 Use the brown color flow icing to pipe bamboo lines on the roof pieces (photo B), and attach the roof.

5 Spread some thinned brown icing on the base, leaving space for a rock garden. Lay a banana chip path, and pour sunflower seeds on the rest of the base. The icing will secure them in place. Pour sugar for the rock garden and rake lines in it with a fork (photo C).

6 Cut the pretzel sticks into rake pieces (photo D). Attach them using icing. Lay the rake in the garden. Construct the arch over the path using the large pretzel sticks and icing.

7 Use icing to make the peanut sculptures (photo E). Settle the sculptures in the sugar rock garden and the yard using icing.

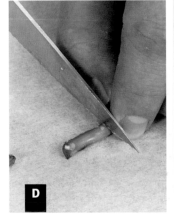

DESIGNER: LEANNE ASH

Country Chapel

You need little more than icing and pumpkin seeds to create a humble chapel and an idyllic scene from days gone by.

WHAT YOU NEED
1 batch gingerbread dough (page 24)
1 batch royal icing (page 24)
Cardboard pattern pieces from the Basic House template (page 76)
Cardboard pattern pieces for the Steeple Base (page 78)
2 handfuls red hard candies
Red, blue, yellow, and green food colors
3 ice cream cones (called sugar cones)
4 handfuls unsalted pumpkin seeds
Several pretzel sticks
1 package graham crackers
4 mini-pretzel squares 2 black jellybeans
6 ladyfinger-style cookies
Extra mixing bowls
Gingerbread cutting tools
Paper towel
Craft awl
Spatula
Knife
Pastry bag with tips

1 Roll out the dough, and use the cutting tools and cardboard patterns to cut out the house pieces. Don't forget to make the pieces for the steeple base. Cut out three arched 1 ¾ x 2 ¼-inch (4.4 x 5.7 cm) windows on the two longest side walls, and one 1 ¼ x 3-inch (3.2 x 7.6 cm) window above the doorway. Bake the house pieces, following the instructions on page 11. Five minutes before the pieces are done, make the melted candy windows, following the instructions on page 19. Allow your chapel pieces to cool.

2 Scratch the outline of a stone pattern into the gingerbread along the bottom 2 inches (5 cm) of all four walls (photo A).

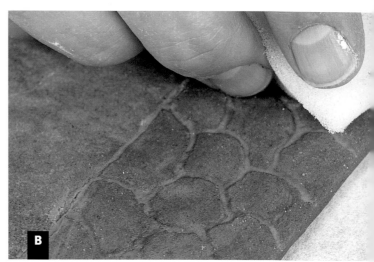

3 Use the food coloring to make a small batch of gray royal icing. Use your fingers or the spatula to smear the icing onto the scratched areas. Wipe away any extra icing with a moist paper towel, so that only the "stonework" crevices are filled (photo B).

4 Spread white icing on the area above the stonework of all four walls. To create the siding, use the knife to draw horizontal lines in the icing (photo C). Color some icing red, and use the pastry bag to pipe a pair of doors on the front wall. Use the knife to draw a line where the doors meet. Allow the icing to harden.

5 Assemble the chapel, following the instructions on page 12. Assemble the steeple base on the roof of the chapel, placing it 2 inches (5 cm) from the edge of the roof nearest the doorway (photo D and Figure 1). The notched pieces will rest on the roof's peak; the square pieces will be attached to them and stand on opposites sides of the roof.

6 Use the pastry bag to pipe white icing on the top of the steeple base. Attach an ice cream cone. Pipe the ice cream cone with icing. Attach the pumpkin seeds as shingles, working in rows from the bottom up (photo E).

7 Spread the gray icing on the roof, and apply pumpkin seeds as shingles, working in rows from the bottom up. Make a cross from pretzels and white icing. When the icing has hardened, attach the cross to the top of the steeple.

8 To build the steps, break two graham crackers into quarters. Lay one piece centered lengthwise below the doorway as a spacing guide. Build the first step in front of the guide, with a riser, a tread, and a support riser, all attached with icing. (This step will look like a bench.) Pick up the guide and use it as the riser to the second step. Use a lot of icing to attach the top tread to the house, just below the doorway, and to the riser (photo F). Use icing to attach two pretzel snaps for the railing.

9 Make a small batch of green icing. Use the pastry bag to pipe this icing under the roofline and along the edges of each window and the doorway. Pipe on door hinges and knobs. Pipe ivy on the stonework.

10 Cover the base with white icing. Cut the cookies so that they have one square edge and stand them up like tombstones in the churchyard. To make the trees, cover two ice cream cones with the green icing. Place them in the churchyard.

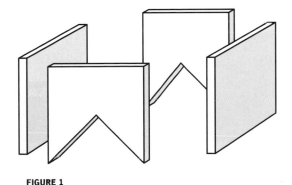

FIGURE 1

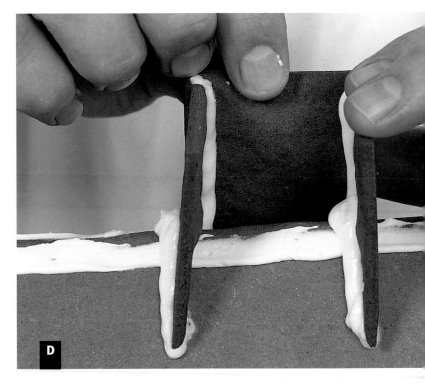

D

E

F

DESIGNER: CATHY STEWART

Pooch Paradise

The sign over the door lets everyone know who's not *welcome in this well-accessorized doggie dream house.*

WHAT YOU NEED
1 batch gingerbread dough (page 24)
1 batch royal icing (page 24)
Cardboard pattern pieces from the Basic House template (page 76)
1 box saltine crackers
12 small pretzel sticks
4 small dog biscuits
Black, brown, and red gel food colors (or colored royal icing)
2 handfuls dried fungus
12 large pretzel sticks
4 handfuls dried guava
4 handfuls parsley
2 handfuls grain cereal
1 batch pastillage (page 000)
2 pinches blue sugar
1 pinch granola
2 decorative basketballs (available in cake decorating shops)
2 decorative baseballs (available in cake decorating shops)
Gingerbread cutting tools
Serrated knife
Spatula

2 Practice laying out the crackers on each wall, using the serrated knife to cut the crackers as needed. Then, spread the royal icing on each wall and press the crackers into the icing, working in rows from the bottom up (photo A).

3 Pipe icing around each window, and press the pretzel sticks into place to create the window framing and trim (photo B).

A

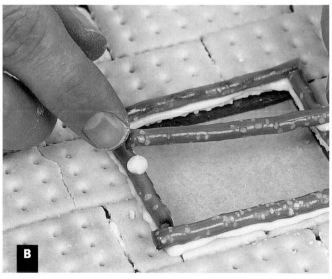

B

1 Roll out the dough, and use the cutting tools and cardboard patterns to cut out the house pieces. Cut one extra 2 x 3-inch (5 x 7.6 cm) piece of gingerbread for the No Cats sign. Cut one 2 ³⁄₄-inch (7 cm) square window from the center of each side wall and one 4 x 3-inch (10.2 x 7.6 cm) arched doorway. Bake the house pieces, following the instructions on page 11, and allow them to cool.

4 Pipe icing onto the back of a dog biscuit and attach it to the side of one window, as a shutter. Pipe extra icing onto the wall beneath the biscuit shutter, if needed (photo C). Repeat with the other biscuits on each side of each window.

5 Spread icing on the sign piece. Allow the icing to dry. Use the black food color gel to draw a cat face in the center of the sign (photo D). Allow the gel to dry.

6 Use the red gel food color to draw a circle around the cat face, and draw a diagonal line through the cat face (photo E). Allow the gel to dry.

7 Assemble just the walls of the house, following the instructions on page 12. Attaching the dried fungus bedding material on the floor using icing, then assemble the roof of the house. Pipe icing onto each corner, and press three large pretzel sticks into each corner to create the decorative supports (photo F). Use icing to attach the No Cats signs above the doorway.

8 Spread icing on the roof, and attach the guava pieces (which look just like bacon-style dog treats) as shingles, working in rows from the bottom up. Attach more pieces on the outside edge of the roof (photo G).

9 Spread icing on the base. Sprinkle parsley for grass and the grain cereal for a path as wide as the doorway. Sculpt the dog accessories from pastillage—a water dish and a food dish—using the instructions on page 22. Sculpt the mushrooms and color them with the brown food color. Fill the water dish with blue sugar and fill the food dish with granola. Place the balls in the yard.

DESIGNER: DIANA LIGHT

Dorothy's House Lands in Oz

Bright colors and delightful details—ruby red slippers, the yellow brick road, Munchkinland trees—bring a classic story to life and create a novel gingerbread house.

1 Roll out the dough, and use the cutting tools and cardboard patterns to cut out the house pieces. Cut one 2-inch (5 cm) square window from each side wall, two 2-inch (5 cm) windows side-by-side from the front wall, and one doorway from the front wall. Save the window and door pieces; you'll re-attach them in step 5. Bake the house pieces (including the windows and door), following the instructions on page 11, and allow them to cool.

2 Sketch the placement of the house and the road on youe base (photo A). Be sure to sketch the road so it has a narrow section, which will show off the color flow you'll create in step 3, and a wide section, which you'll pave in step 3.

3 Use the instructions on page 19 to make and apply color flow to the narrow section of the road (photo B). (One part red to three parts yellow makes bright orange.) Cut the tips off the candy corn, then make yellow color flow. Working in sections, apply yellow color flow to the wide part of the road and pave it with the remaining candy corn pieces. (You don't want the icing to dry before you attach the candy corn.) Make a gray color flow (mixing green, yellow, and red color), and cover the rest of the base with it. Allow the icing to dry.

4 Working in rows from the bottom up, use either the leftover green icing or white icing to attach the gum to the house walls. (The icing won't be visible.) Leave spaces to make it appear that the gum "siding" was blown off when the twister picked up the house. Attach the windows askew, using white icing.

5 Assemble the house, following the instructions on page 12. Repeat step 5 to attach the gum pieces to the roof, slightly overlapping the shingles (photo C). Leave some blank spaces.

6 Skewer the gumdrops with the lollipops to make lollipop trees (photo D).

7 Break the licorice stick into two pieces, and make the witch's legs poking out from under the house near the front windows. To make the ruby red slippers, cover two candy corns with icing, and then roll each in the red sugar sprinkles (photo E). Place the slippers at the ends of the legs. Pour the rainbow sprinkles around the yellow brick road and in the yard, as shown.

Tropical Tiki Hut

Forget icicles and snow—think bamboo and sand and reveling on a Polynesian beach before carved tiki gods and blazing tiki torches.

DESIGNER: CATHY STEWART

1 batch gingerbread dough (page 24)

1 batch royal icing (page 24)

Cardboard pattern pieces from the Basic House template (page 76)

Peach and red food colors

1 bag small pretzel sticks

6 sugar fish

1 package sesame bars

15 large pretzel sticks

10 Necco wafers

2 large cinnamon sticks

5 candy cola bottles

25 green Gummy strips

24 pieces of thin pasta

1 dried star anise

6 candy melon slices

1 red Gummy strip

5 reception sticks

2 handfuls of tri-color orzo

3 lemon sugar cookies

4 candy starfish

2 candy seahorses

Gingerbread cutting tools

Spatula

Serrated knife

Pastry bag and tips

Thick kitchen towel

1 Roll out the dough and use the cutting tools and cardboard patterns to cut out the house pieces, plus one extra side wall piece. Cut away a 6 x 3-inch (15.2 x 7.6 cm) arched doorway from each end wall, as shown in the main project photo. The tiki hut has two reach-through bar areas, which have interior and exterior walls and countertops cut from what would normally be side wall pieces (see figure 1). Horizontal roof supports provide stability but aren't visible in the finished tiki hut. Cut two bar wall pieces (10 x 3 inches [25.4 x 7.6 cm] each) and two roof supports (10 x 1/2 inches [26.7 cm] each) from each of two side walls. Cut two countertop pieces (10 x 2 inch [25.4 x 5 cm] each) from the third side wall piece. Bake the tiki hut pieces, following the instructions on page 11, and allow them to cool. Set the roof supports aside.

2 Use the food color to make all the royal icing peach colored. Spread icing on the two end walls, to color the interior walls. Allow the icing to harden, then flip the walls over.

3 To make the bamboo siding, use the serrated knife to cut the small pretzels into a variety of lengths. Working in sections, spread icing on the wall pieces, including the interior and exterior bar walls, and press the pretzels into place. Stagger them, as shown. Use the icing to attach three fish above each exterior doorway. Allow the icing to harden.

A

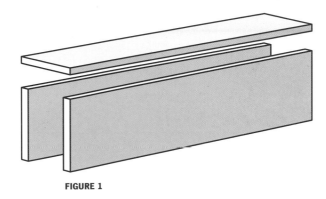

FIGURE 1

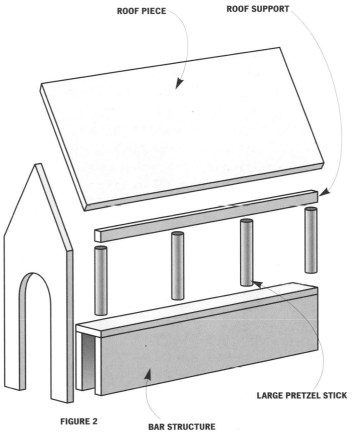

ROOF PIECE

ROOF SUPPORT

LARGE PRETZEL STICK

FIGURE 2

BAR STRUCTURE

4 Using the basic building instructions on page 11 as a guide, assemble the bar structure (again, see figure 1) and the end walls.

5 Attach the sesame bars to the countertops with icing, and edge them with small pretzel sticks. To make the tiki god roof supports, trim eight of the large pretzel sticks to fit between the countertop and the roof supports (refer to figure 2). Then use the serrated knife to carve a face into four of the large pretzel sticks. For ease and to avoid injury, hold each pretzel in a thick kitchen towel as you use the other hand to carve. Put red food color into the features (photo A). Use icing to attach the large pretzels for supports as shown, putting the four tiki god faces on the front of your tiki hut.

6 Attach the roof supports by placing one roof support lengthwise atop the tiki gods on each side. Attach the roof pieces using the basic instructions on page 12 (again see figure 2).

7 To make the stacked trays, alternate the Necco wafers and icing. Mount these and the cola bottles on the countertops. Make serving trays by attaching the small candies to more Necco wafers, and then attach the wafers to the countertops.

8 Use a generous amount of icing to hang fruit slices to the underside of the roof supports, as shown in the main project photo.

9 Notch the green Gummy strips to create a leafy pattern (photo B). Use icing to attach the candy greenery to the roof, working in rows from the bottom up so there is overlap. Divide each side of the roof into three spaces with rows of four pasta pieces. Attach the cinnamon sticks to the peak of the roof, then attach one dried star anise in the center.

10 Spread icing on your base. Make the bamboo bar stools by cutting two long pretzels sticks in half, covering three of them with the icing, and then pressing the small pretzel sticks into the icing (photo C). Use extra icing to stand the bar stools near the bar. Top each stool with a cookie.

11 Sprinkle the orzo on top of the base. Create the tiki torches by cutting the red Gummy strip for flames and attaching them to the tips of each of the reception sticks (photo D). Stand the torches in your base. For support, break the remaining large pretzels into 1 to 2 inch (2.5 to 5 cm) pieces, and stack them in front of and behind the torches, as shown. Cover the supports with icing, and place two starfish and one seahorse near the base of each torch.

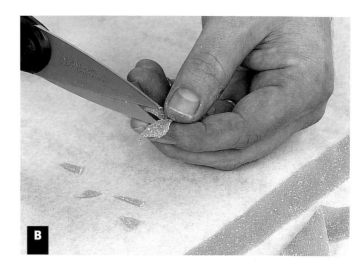

B

C

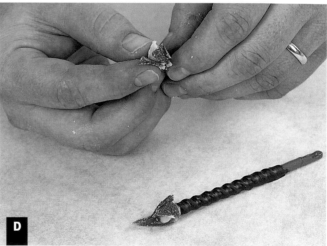

D

DESIGNER: ROSE REITZEL-PERRY

Treetop Playhouse

Build the tree fort you always wanted, and stock it with toys and books; a simple support structure lets you leave one wall open.

WHAT YOU NEED

1 batch gingerbread dough (page 24)

1 batch royal icing (page 24)

Cardboard pattern pieces from the Basic House template (page 76)

Two 8 x 14-inch (20 x 36 cm) plywood bases (optional)

Crotch of a small tree branch (optional)

1 bag pretzel squares

12 rectangular wafer cookies

6 large pretzel rods

3 fruit roll ups

Several small pretzel sticks

6 pieces chewy fruit candy

6 large pretzel sticks

1 pack square chewing gum

3 caramels

4 gumdrops

30 Red Hots

Gingerbread cutting tools

Spatula

Pastry bag and tips

Scissors

Straight pin

BASE NOTE: To create the treetop look, cut an extra, identical base from wood and find a branch that fits the base in its crotch. Plane the branch ends and screw the branch to the extra base, using at least two screws so it doesn't pivot. Figure out how your house base will sit in the branches, and mark at least three points of contact. Put short, flat-head screws into the branches, so the tree house will rest on the screw heads. Test your treetop base by settling the house base onto it and piling a few heavy books on top.

1 Roll out the dough, and use the cutting tools and cardboard patterns to cut out the house pieces. To create the open wall, you'll cut the front wall into four strips measuring ½ inch (1.3 cm) wide and 7 inches (17.8 cm) long, and one strip measuring ½ inch (1.3

cm) wide and 6 inches (15.2 cm) long. These will be the roof supports, as shown in the main project photo. Bake the house pieces and supports, following the instructions on page 11, and allow them to cool.

2 Cover the exterior back wall with royal icing, and shingle it by pressing the pretzel squares into the icing, working in rows from the bottom up. Repeat for the end walls, but at the height of the horizontal roof edge make one row of pretzels overhang those below (photo A). Allow the icing to harden.

3 Create one window on each exterior wall by attaching three wafer cookies, one at a time, side-by-side in the center of each wall. For a secure attachment, pipe the icing on the back of the wafer, and then press it into the pretzel-covered wall (photo B). Allow the icing to harden.

4 Erect the three walls, using the basic instructions on page 12. Attach one of the 7-inch (17.8 cm) supports in the left front corner of the open side of the

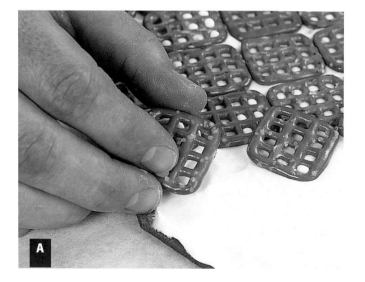

A

B

C

E

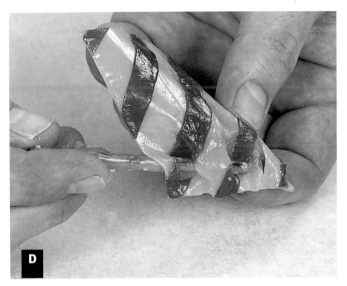

D

with edibility, leave the plastic on. It won't show, and it makes the fruit roll ups easier to work with.) You can pattern your flag with stripes or polka dots cut from another fruit roll up. Thread a pretzel stick through the slots for a curtain rod or flag pole (photo D). Use icing to attach the curtain rods and curtains to the interior walls, matching up with where you hung your shutters on the exterior.

6 Make presents by stacking fruit chews and giving them a fruit roll up bow, using the instructions on page 20. Make books by wrapping gum around caramels. Dip a straight pin into blue or black food coloring, and press it against the spine of the book to simulate writing. Use icing to place the presents, books, and gumballs inside the tree house.

house. Use icing to attach a pretzel rod (cut to length) to each of the remaining 7-inch (17.8 cm) upright supports. Allow the icing to harden, then flip the three supports over and space them evenly before attaching the shorter support across them (photo C). Allow the icing to harden, then attach the support structure in the right side of the open side of the tree house so that the pretzels face the house, as shown in the main project photo. Use a liberal amount of icing.

7 Attach the roof, using the instructions on page 14. Allow the icing to harden. Use icing to attach one large pretzel rod to each outside corner, for added stability.

8 Shingle your roof with the round crackers, working in rows, attaching the crackers with icing from the bottom up. Use icing to attach two large pretzel rods to the roofline, and flank them with pretzel sticks. Make holly swags by cutting a gumdrop in half and pinching the skinny end in on itself to a point (photo E) to form the leaves. Use Red Hots as the berries, attaching them and the leaves to the center of the roofline, the side of each roof peak, the base of each corner, the top of each exterior window, and anywhere else you like. Use any leftover icing to cover the base and put "snow" in the tree branches.

5 Line the interior of the house with wafer cookies, cutting them to fit. Finish the seams with pretzel rods; they look good and provide stability. Make curtains and a flag by cutting ¼-inch (6 mm) slits vertically along the top of fruit roll ups, about 1 inch (2.5 cm) apart. Make the cuts with scissors before you peel off the plastic backing. (If you're not concerned

Dome Sweet Dome

*You don't have to be a North Pole native to make this easy-as-pie igloo
or to sculpt the playful pastillage penguins.*

DESIGNER: NATHALIE MORNU

WHAT YOU NEED

½ batch of gingerbread dough (page 24)

1 batch of royal icing (page 24)

Two tablespoons of vegetable oil

½ batch fondant (page 24)

2 bags sugar cubes

Blue, red, green, and black food colors

½ batch pastillage (page 24) (optional)

1 fruit roll up (optional)

Medium-sized mixing bowl

Cookie sheet

Aluminum foil

Gingerbread cutting tools

Empty small vegetable can

Spatula

Pastry bag and tips

Knife

Wax paper

1 Turn your mixing bowl upside down on a cookie sheet, cover it with aluminum foil, and coat the foil with the oil. Roll out the dough to a piece that's large enough to cover the bowl. (This igloo's dome is 12 inches [30.5 cm] in diameter.) Lay the dough over the bowl (photo A). Cut away excess dough. Cut an opening for your tunnel, then bake the gingerbread in place on the inverted bowl, following the instructions on page 11, and allow it to cool. Gently remove the cooled igloo shape from the inverted bowl, and place it on your base.

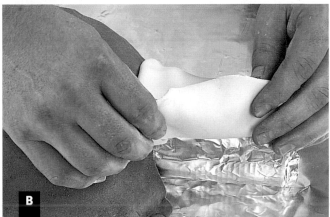

2 To make the tunnel, wrap the exterior of the can with aluminum foil, and coat the foil with the oil. Oil your work surface lightly, and roll out some fondant so you have a piece large enough to drape over the can with overlap onto the base and the side of the igloo (photo B).

3 Press the fondant onto the can, and use your fingers to press it onto the gingerbread. Where the bottom of the tunnel meets the base, press the fondant onto the base. Cut off excess fondant. Allow the fondant to harden.

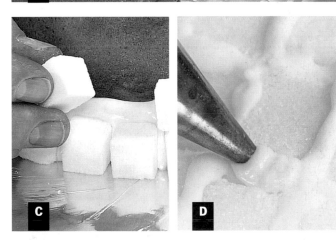

4 Working in rows from the bottom up, apply royal icing to the igloo and attach sugar cubes to it (photo C). Use the knife to gently saw some sugar cubes to a size that will fit any small gaps. Gently apply icing to one side of the fondant tunnel, and attach sugar cubes the same way.

5 Use the pastry bag to pipe icing along all the gaps between the sugar cubes (photo D).

6 Gently remove the can from the tunnel (photo E). Cover the base with icing. Mix a small batch of royal icing and create the pond.

7 Make the wreath using the instructions on page 20. Attach it with icing. Purchase ready-made penguins from a cake or pastry decorating shop, or shape them from pastillage, following the instructions on page 22. Make a scarf for each penguin by cutting two strips of fruit roll up, tying one piece around each penguin's neck. Attach them with icing, if necessary.

Majestic Mariner's Lighthouse

Use just one set of specialty templates to make this picturesque display of an elegant, lonely tower atop a rocky shore.

DESIGNER: NATHALIE MORNU

WHAT YOU NEED

1 batch gingerbread dough (page 24)

1 batch royal icing (page 24)

Cardboard pattern pieces from the Lighthouse template (page 78)

1 package cinnamon rice cakes

2 tablespoons cooking oil

2 batches fondant (page 24)

1 small jar apricot preserves [optional]

Black and blue food colors

One 3-inch (7.6 cm) round cookie or gingerbread piece

4 sheets leaf gelatin

1 yellow hard candy

6 pieces licorice twists

1 handful jellybean stones

Gingerbread cutting tools

Pastry bag and tips

Rolling pin

Spatula

Basting brush

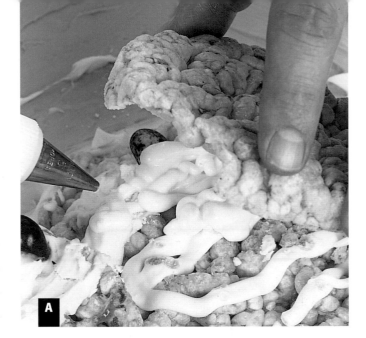

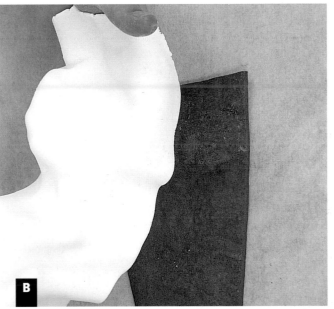

1 Roll out the dough, and use the cutting tools and cardboard pattern to cut out the lighthouse pieces. Bake the lighthouse pieces, following the instructions on page 11, and then allow them to cool.

2 Make the "rocky" shore upon which the lighthouse will stand. Build a platform of three layers of rice cakes, breaking them as needed so they'll fit closely together. Attach them to the base and to each other with royal icing (photo A).

3 Lay out your wall pieces. Apply a light coat of oil to your work surface, and then roll out enough fondant to cover one wall completely. Place the fondant atop a wall piece (photo B) and cut around it, leaving ½ inch (1.3 cm) extra around all sides (photo C).

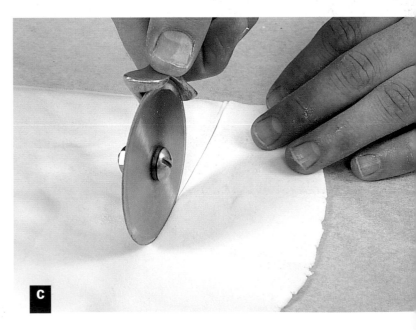

4 Warm some apricot preserves so they're slightly runny (they shouldn't be uncomfortable to dip your finger into), and gently brush a thin coat of preserves onto a wall of the lighthouse. (For an extra sturdy lighthouse, you could substitute icing for preserves.) Support the fondant so it doesn't stretch as you press it gently against the gingerbread. Repeat to cover the other three walls.

5 Add the black food coloring to the remaining fondant. On a lightly oiled surface, roll out enough black fondant to cut into stripes that will wrap around the walls and to cover the square gingerbread piece that serves as the roof of the lighthouse. Cut strips of black fondant. Apply warm preserves (or icing) to the backs of the strips, and apply the strips to the walls (photo D). Using warm preserves to secure it in place, wrap black fondant around the flat roof piece, wrapping it 1 inch (2.5 cm) under the gingerbread. Cut away excess material. Use your fingers to press the fondant against the gingerbread.

6 Assemble the lighthouse, following the basic instructions on page 11. Though your lighthouse looks different from the basic house, the basic building techniques for attaching four walls to one another will guarantee you a sturdy, freestanding structure. Attach the roof piece. Use extra icing to secure the lighthouse to the rice cake foundation.

7 For the lamp, use a blob of icing to secure the yellow hard candy in the center of the observation deck. For the observatory windows, cut out five equally sized pieces of leaf gelatin. Place them upright on the black fondant roof in a circular shape, making sure all edges meet. Press their bottom edges into the fondant to help keep them in place. Mix up some black icing and pipe it along all the seams of the gelatin leaf (photo E), and reinforce the top edge of the circular structure with more piped icing.

8 In the corners of the roof, gently press short pieces of licorice into the fondant to act as railing supports. Secure them with black icing. Allow the entire roof structure to harden completely.

D

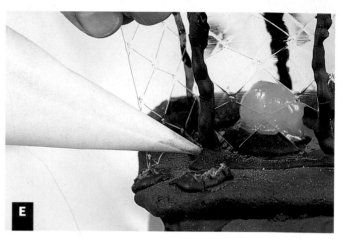

E

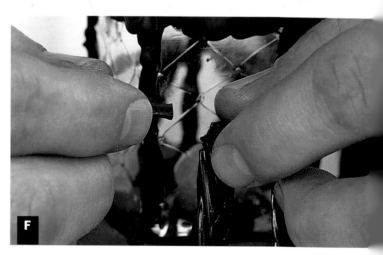

F

9 Place the cookie atop the observation deck, using black icing to attach it as well as to cover the top of it. Allow the icing to harden. Roll a small ball of black fondant, and attach it to the top of the roof with black icing. Cut the licorice rope into quarters down its length. Using black icing, attach the licorice to the railing supports (photo F).

10 Cut the jellybeans in half. Attach them randomly around the rice cake base with icing. Create the ocean by making blue icing and spreading it on the base. Create the whitecaps with dabs of white icing, applied with the basting brush.

DESIGNER: CARROLL DOUGALL

Medieval Castle

*Imagine the heroic battles and splendid pageants hosted
in this formidable fortress as you easily construct
its four towers from one template.*

WHAT YOU NEED

1 batch gingerbread dough (page 24)

1 batch royal icing (page 24)

Cardboard pattern pieces from the Basic House template, modified to cut the peak off the end wall pieces, minus the roof pieces (page 76)

Cardboard pattern piece for the Castle Roof template (page 76)

Cardboard pattern pieces from the Chimney template, plus an extra front piece, minus the notched roof piece (page 76)

White modeling chocolate

4 handfuls chocolate rocks

12 Tootsie Rolls

Red, yellow, and blue food colors

2 pieces black licorice

10 Necco Wafers in various colors

1 candy crest

2 rainbow color sucker poles

Gingerbread cutting tools

Extra mixing bowls

Paper towel

Pastry bag and tips

1 Roll out the dough, and use the cutting tools and cardboard patterns to cut out the house and chimney pieces. Be sure to cut the peaks off the end walls. Bake the pieces, following the instructions on page 11, and allow them to cool.

2 Assemble the castle, following the basic instructions on page 12. Though your castle looks different from the basic house, the basic building techniques for attaching four walls to one another will guarantee you a sturdy, freestanding structure. Attach the towers by attaching the extra front piece to a corner of the castle, then attaching a side piece (photo A). Then add the other side piece and the front piece, to complete the tower.

3 Brush the white chocolate onto the walls of the castle with a paper towel to create a weathered stone effect (photo B).

4 Use the pastry bag to pipe royal icing to the base of one tower, and begin attaching the chocolate rocks on the wall, working from the bottom up (photo C). Repeat for the other towers.

5 To create the tops of the towers, cut the Tootsie Rolls in half and flatten them between your fingers. Use icing to attach three to each side of one of the tower tops (photo D). Repeat for the other towers.

6 To make the door, color some icing brown and pipe it on the door to resemble a vertical wood grain. Heat one piece of licorice in a microwave for 15 seconds, to make it pliable. Stretch it, bend it, and apply it as the door frame. Microwave the other licorice piece, then cut it into pieces and make the door handles and hinges. Attach them using the brown icing.

7 Spread white icing on the base. Create a path as wide as the doorway by breaking the Necco Wafers into pieces. Alternately lay them and chocolate rocks in the icing (photo E). Stand the two sucker poles on opposite sides of the path, using extra icing to secure them. Use icing to mount a crest above the doorway.

8 Color a small amount of the icing green, and use the small tip to pipe leaves and ivy on the left and right walls of the castle. Then color a small amount of the icing red, and use the star tip to pipe flowers between the leaves. Use yellow icing for the flower centers (photo F).

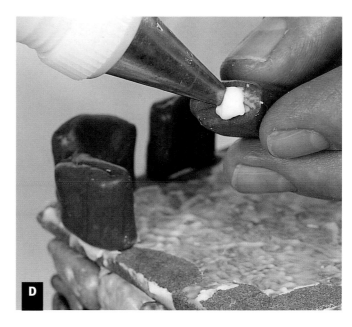

D

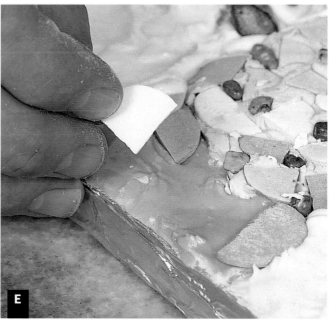

E

C

F

DESIGNER: LANCE B. ETHRIDGE, SR.

High Noon Saloon

*Make a faux two-story saloon, complete with wagon-wheel swinging doors, a trusty horse,
and a side staircase for quick escapes.*

WHAT YOU NEED

1 batch gingerbread dough (page 24)

1 batch royal icing (page 24)

Cardboard pattern pieces from the Basic House template (page 76)

Cardboard pattern pieces from the Escape Stairs templates (page 77)

2 pasta wheels

1 package white modeling chocolate

3 pieces red licorice twists

1 package brown modeling chocolate

8 short pretzel sticks

Red and brown oil-based or powdered food colors

4 peppermint sticks

1 pack red, short-sticked chewing gum

3 chocolate cigarettes

1 box Honey Graham squares

1 bag brown sugar

4 Tootsie Rolls

1 large flake shredded wheat cereal

Green oil-based or powdered food color

Gingerbread cutting tools

Extra cardboard

Piping bag and tips

Wax paper

Mixing bowl

Medium paintbrush or pastry brush

Cactus-shaped chocolate mold

Horse-shaped chocolate mold

1 Roll out the dough, and use the cutting tools and cardboard patterns to cut out the saloon pieces. Cut a 2 x 4-inch (5 x 10.2 cm) doorway in the center of the front wall piece. Reduce front doorway cutout to make two swinging doors. Press one pasta wheel on each swinging door piece. Bake the house pieces, including the swinging doors, following the instructions on page 11, and allow them to cool.

2 To make the chocolate windows, cut three 2-inch square (5 cm) pieces of cardboard (for the "second-story" windows) and two 3-inch (7.6 cm) squares (to flank the swinging doors). Lay them on the wax paper. Heat the white chocolate for 30 seconds in a microwave, then pour it over each cardboard piece. Allow the chocolate to set.

3 Pull the strands from the licorice and cut them into three pieces, matching the length to the window sides. There should be six sets of licorice for the top saloon windows. Place the licorice in the microwave and heat for 10 seconds. Pinch the centers and form a curtain appearance. Spread the strands, place them on the cooling chocolate windows, and trim them (photo A).

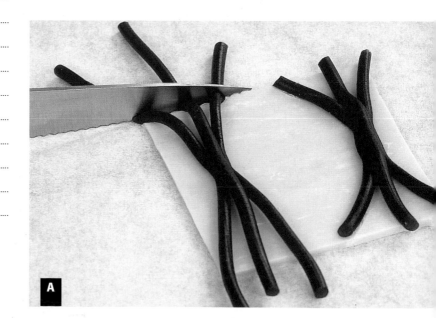

A

4 When the chocolate is completely set, pipe dark chocolate crosses in each window (photo B). On the lower chocolate windows place pretzels to form a cross. Allow the chocolate to set. Tint some royal icing with red food coloring, and pipe the icing in between each licorice strand to finish the curtains.

5 Assemble the walls of the saloon, using the basic instructions on page 12. Attach the two stringers for your staircase using icing and the supports (photo C), but don't attach the staircase to the saloon wall yet. Allow the icing to harden. Wait to attach the porch, escape door, and stair roof. In the meantime, use a knife to carefully loosen the windows from their cardboard templates. Attach the windows to the saloon using icing. Frame each first-floor window by attaching pretzel sticks with icing, and attach a row of additional pretzel sticks above these windows, to help support the porch roof, which you'll attach next.

6 Using peppermint sticks for porch supports, attach the porch, using the instructions on page 12. Use icing to attach the escape door stairs, and then attach the gum pieces as stair treads. Use icing to attach the escape door, and then attach the stair roof. Place a chocolate cigarette under the left corner for support. (The right corner is supported by the open door.)

7 Working in rows beginning at the lower left edge of the roof, use icing to attach the Honey Graham Squares to the roof, porch overhang, and stair roof. Place the successive rows slightly off-center, to achieve a shingled look.

8 Attach the saloon doors using icing. Prop the doors in place until they dry. Color some of the icing brown, and apply it to the walls of the saloon. Before the icing dries, dab the bristles of the paintbrush or pastry brush into the icing, giving it a stucco effect.

9 Cover the base with icing, and sprinkle brown sugar for the ground. Brush some extra sugar up near the saloon to give it the appearance of drifted dirt. To make the two hitching posts, shape four Tootsie Rolls into two pairs of short posts. Notch one end of

B

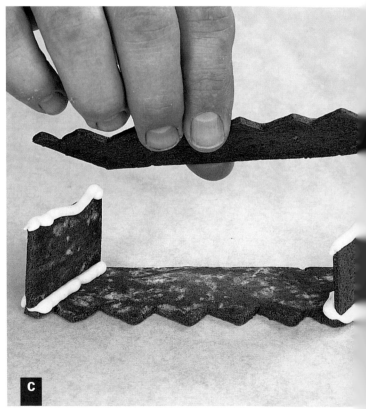

C

each post with your finger, and place half a chocolate cigarette into each notch. Use icing to attach one hitching post on the "ground" in front of each large window.

10 Make tumbleweeds by breaking apart the Shredded Wheat and sticking individual pieces into mounds of icing (photo D).

11 Separate the white and brown chocolate into three batches. Heat them in the microwave oven until they're melted. Add green food color to one white batch and pour into the cactus form. Pipe some brown chocolate into the horse mold for the mane, saddle stirrups, and the tail. Then pipe the rest of the white chocolate into the mold (photo E). Allow the chocolates to set, then remove them from each mold.

12 Attach the cactus just behind the stairs and the horse to the right side of the right hitching post. To tie your horse to the hitching post, roll a Tootsie Roll into a rope shape. Press one end on the horse's harness; drape the other on the hitching post.

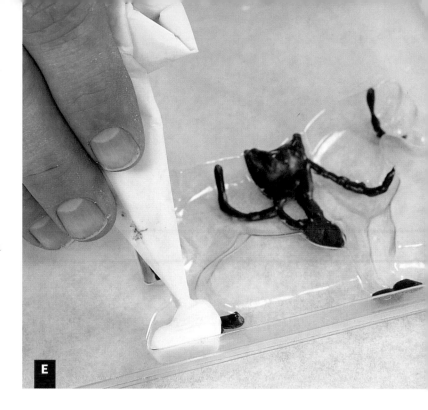

DESIGNER: CHRISTINA PRATICO BANNER

Classic Victorian

Slightly taller walls and architectural details create the illusion of a two-story house, but this gorgeous Victorian uses the basic recipe and techniques.

WHAT YOU NEED

1 batch gingerbread dough (page 24)

1 batch royal icing (page 24)

Cardboard pattern pieces from the Classic Victorian template (page 79)

Green, blue, and yellow food colors

4 packs of long, red gum sticks

1 box regular Necco wafers

4 tablespoons light corn syrup

1 box of Pez candies

3 boxes white breath mints

12 peppermint sticks

3 mini pretzel squares

12 round peppermint candies

4 Hershey's Kisses

2 chocolate chips

2 bags shredded coconut

1 box snack cakes

2 pretzel sticks

2 chocolate truffles

2 miniature Reese's Peanut Butter Cups

2 gumballs

2 chocolate sticks

2 butterscotch candies

2 Rolos

4 red fruit roll ups

1 handful white sugar

2 tablespoons white edible glitter

Gingerbread cutting tools

Pastry bag and tip

Wax paper

FIGURE 1

1 This house has one extra roof piece, but the house is made using the same techniques as any gingerbread house. Roll out the dough, and use the cutting tools and cardboard patterns to cut out the house pieces. Remember to cut the 1-inch tip off both peaked end walls. Bake the house pieces, following the instructions on page 11, and allow them to cool.

2 Use food color and the color flow instructions on page 19 to draw on the windows and the door in the style and sizes you choose. (This house features color flow curtains in most windows. The windows range from 1 inch [2.5 cm] to 3 inches [7.6 cm] wide, and 1 ½ inches [3.8 cm] to 3 inches [7.6 cm] tall.) Allow the windows to dry. Cut the gum into thin strips and attach them as door and window trim and frames, using the royal icing (photo A). Allow the icing to harden.

3 Assemble the walls of the house, following the basic instructions on page 12. When you're ready to attach the roof, place the 13 ½ x 1 ½-inch (34.3 x 3.8 cm) "roof peak" piece horizontally on the peak points. Then attach the two remaining roof pieces. Attach the dormer, following the instructions on page 15.

4 Attach the Necco wafers to the roof with icing, starting from the bottom edge and overlapping the wafers (photo B). Break some in half to edge the ends and top, as well as to create the decorative detail halfway up the sides of the house. Lightly brush the wafers with light corn syrup thinned with a few drops of water. (This makes the surface gleam.)

5 Using icing, apply two rows of Pez candies to the base of the walls, and form the steps and path with more Pez. To create the trim, use icing to attach white breath mints in a pattern as shown in figure 1 (page 69), below the roof, at the top of the dormer windows, and horizontally along the center of the walls (photo C).

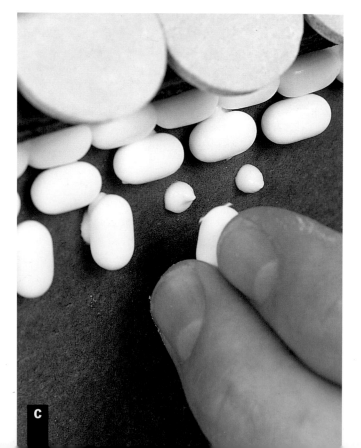

6 For decoration on each corner and to cover where the house pieces come together, attach a peppermint stick with icing (photo D). You'll need two sticks per corner, stacked vertically.

7 Spread icing on top of the roof and in front of the dormer window and attach the standing pretzel

railings to the dormer stoop and along the outside edges of the roof peak piece. Break peppermint sticks to the desired length, and attach a piece at each corner of the railing in front of the dormer window. Top each with a chocolate chip. Use icing to stack three round peppermint candies at each corner of the rooftop. Top each stack with a Hershey's Kiss.

8 Make the hedges by stacking the snack cakes two-high around the edge of the base. Then top them with greenery made from the green food coloring and coconut, following the instructions on page 21. To make topiaries, insert one end of a pretzel stick into a chocolate truffle. Cover the truffle with the greenery mix. Insert the other end of the pretzel stick into an upside-down miniature Reese's Peanut Butter Cup. Place the topiaries on each side of the front door. Cover the large gumballs with coconut greenery to make bushes. Place them on either side of the hedge entrance.

9 Make the wreaths and swags, following the instructions on page 20.

10 To make the lamppost bases, cut snack cakes to the desired size, and use icing to attach one to either side of the hedge entrance. Insert a chocolate stick into the center of each snack cake. Use the icing to surround the base of the lamppost with Pez candies (photo E).

11 Attach a butterscotch candy to the top of the stick with icing, and attach an upside-down Rolo to the top of the candy. Make bows from the fruit roll ups, following the instructions on page 20. Use icing to attach a bow to each lamppost (photo F). Attach the other bows to the wreaths and roofline, as shown in the main project photo.

12 To make snow, blend three parts sugar to one part coconut flakes in a food processor until very fine. Add a little white edible glitter for sparkle. Dampen the edges of some of the Necco wafers so that the snow will stick, and sprinkle them with snow. Sprinkle more snow on the railings, the top of the roof, and the hedges. Spread white icing on the base surrounding the house, and immediately sprinkle it with snow.

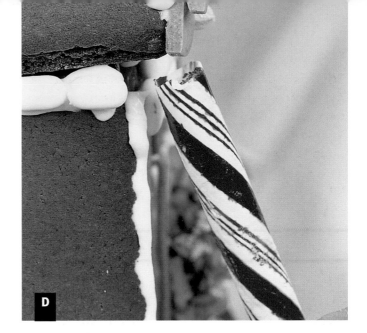

D

E

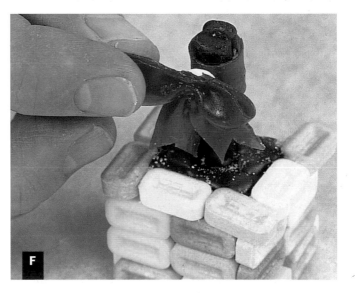

F

DESIGNER: ELIZABETH M. PRIOLI

Santa's Workshop

Santa's making a list and the elves are at work in this traditional scene. You can make or purchase the pastillage figures and accessories.

1 batch gingerbread dough (Page 24) (To achieve the light color, substitute white sugar for brown sugar, or corn syrup for molasses. Omitting the molasses will affect the flavor and aroma more than omitting the brown sugar.)

2 batches royal icing (page 24)

2 batches pastillage (page 24)

Cardboard pattern pieces from the Basic House template, minus one roof piece (page 76)

Cardboard pattern pieces from the Santa's Workshop templates (page 78)

2-inch-deep (5 cm) polystyrene base (optional)

Red, yellow, blue, and brown food colors

8 graham crackers

40 small red heart candies

40 medium red candies

4 packs rectangular snack crackers

2 packages miniature white, red, and green decorative candies

2 packages white, red, and green sprinkles

30 thin wheat crackers

1 handful chocolate rocks

1 box mini Chiklets

1 bag shredded coconut

25 miniature candy ornaments

3 miniature candy candles

1 package red licorice

4 Rice Krispy Treats

1 handful mixed dried herbs (parsley, peppermint, alfalfa)

20 sugar cubes

10 square chewable candies

Your choice of food coloring markers

Readymade balls, dolls, sacks, elves, and Santa figures (optional)

15 small pretzel sticks

1 piece black string licorice

1 box confectioner's sugar

Gingerbread cutting tools

Extra mixing bowls

Paper towel

Cardboard, foam, or other temporary supports

Knife

Wax paper

BASE NOTE: If you are using a polystyrene base, use a knife to shape the landscape. Create a level bowl area for the house, but leave a ½-inch-high (1.3 cm) shelf for the house's raised inside step.

1 Roll out the dough, and use the gingerbread cutting tools and cardboard patterns to cut out the house pieces. (Cut the Roof Supports from one of the Side Wall pieces from the Basic House template.) Cut three windows from the front wall, as shown in the main project photo, and two windows of the same size and location from each peaked end wall. Bake the house pieces, following the instructions on page 11, and allow them to cool.

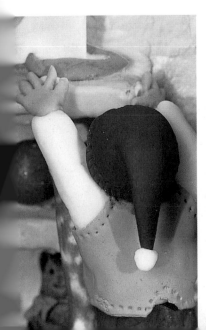

2 Make a colored batch of royal icing, and spread it on the interior of each wall, texturizing it like stucco with a moist paper towel. (The designer used a pale yellow color.) Cut graham crackers to fit for the interior shelves. Paint them with the icing you used on your interior walls. Allow all the icing to dry.

3 Make a batch of brown pastillage. Roll it out thin, and cut out two pieces for your door (for inside and outside), approximately 4 x 2 ½ inches (10.2 x 6.4 cm) each. Trace closely spaced vertical lines in them, and use icing to attach them to the house. For the trim cut approximately 40 ¼-inch strips from the remaining brown pastillage. Begin laying strips on the exterior wall sides in the pattern indicated, spacing them evenly (photo A). Continue the outermost strip to the roofline on each edge of the house. Attach the strips using icing. Make a batch of green pastillage and use it to frame the door and windows on both sides of the walls. Allow the icing to harden.

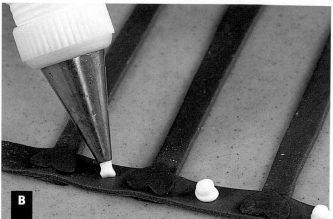

4 Alternate the red heart candies with dots of the royal icing along the vertical strips of brown pastillage (photo B). Attach the medium red candy pieces in the shape of poinsettas on either side of each exterior window and on the door. Pipe a dot of royal icing into each flower center. Allow the royal icing to harden.

5 Assemble the walls and roof supports, following the basic instructions on page 12. Make a batch of pastillage for the chimney and chimney stack. Shape it into stones, press them together, use a knife to distress the surface, then paint with the food colors (photo C). Wipe away excess color with a paper towel. This leaves color in the crevices for a marbled effect.

6 Use extra icing to attach the small red heart candies in a vertical row on the front interior wall, and use the decorative candies and sprinkles to make one flower beneath each window and a row of flowers along each roof support, as shown. Build the raised step that leads to the inside door from the rectangular snack crackers, cutting the crackers to fit. Cover with the "stucco" colored royal icing. Attach the hanging shelves with the same royal icing, and pipe an extra thick line of icing below the shelves to support them. Support the shelves with pieces of cardboard or foam until the icing hardens. Make the rugs by laying mini Chiklets in a bed of icing atop a sheet of wax paper.

When dry, transfer the rugs to your floors, and add an icing fringe.

7 Construct a hearth from the graham crackers. Outline the mantle with brown icing or leftover brown pastillage. Attach some chocolate rocks to the sides of the hearth. Cut the Wheat Thins to fit the interior floor then attach them using the icing.

8 Make the wreaths and swags, following the instructions on page 20.

9 Make the trees and shrubs by combining the Rice Krispy Treats with green icing, and then sprinkling them with a mixture of dried herbs. Decorate the Christmas tree with the candy ornaments (photo D).

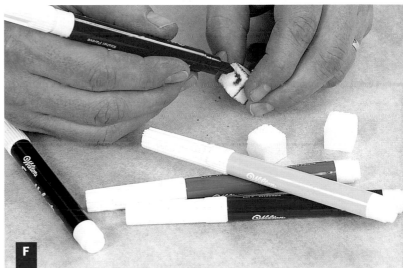

Place it in the house, place the trees and shrubs in the yard, and place one swag in each window, as shown. Place one candy candle in the center of each swag.

10 Cover the inside of the roof pieces with icing, for a white ceiling. Attach the roof. Cut the red licorice pieces in half lengthwise for the roofing, and practice laying out the pattern shown. When you're sure of your placement, attach the licorice to the roof using icing, working in rows from the bottom up (photo E).

11 Make the gift packages by stacking sugar cubes or square chewable candies with icing, and then painting them with colored icing. Make the alphabet cubes by lettering the cubes with food coloring markers (photo F).

12 Purchase ready-made balls, dolls, sacks, elves, and Santa figures from a cake decorating shop, or shape them from pastillage, following the instructions on page 22.

13 Make the two ladders and the fence posts using the pretzel sticks and icing. Use string licorice for the fence rope. Make a small amount of black icing and pipe on door hinges and a door handle. Make the wreath using the instructions on page 20. Pipe a ribbon on using red icing. Attach the wreath to the doorway with icing. Pipe icing as snow on the roof line then sprinkle the house with confectioners sugar to imitate freshly fallen snow.

Templates

*Mark these shapes on cardboard,
using the dimensions provided.*

BASIC HOUSE

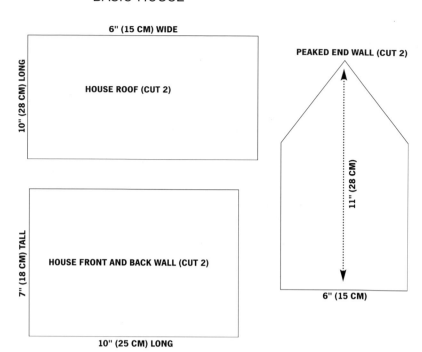

6" (15 CM) WIDE

10" (28 CM) LONG

HOUSE ROOF (CUT 2)

7" (18 CM) TALL

HOUSE FRONT AND BACK WALL (CUT 2)

10" (25 CM) LONG

PEAKED END WALL (CUT 2)

11" (28 CM)

6" (15 CM)

CHIMNEY

FRONT PIECE

SIDE SUPPORT PIECE (CUT 2)

2" (5 CM)

NOTCHED ROOF PIECE

1" (2.5 CM)

12" (30 CM)

12" (30 CM)

2" (5 CM)

1" (2.5 CM)

PUEBLO PERFECT/MEDIEVAL CASTLE

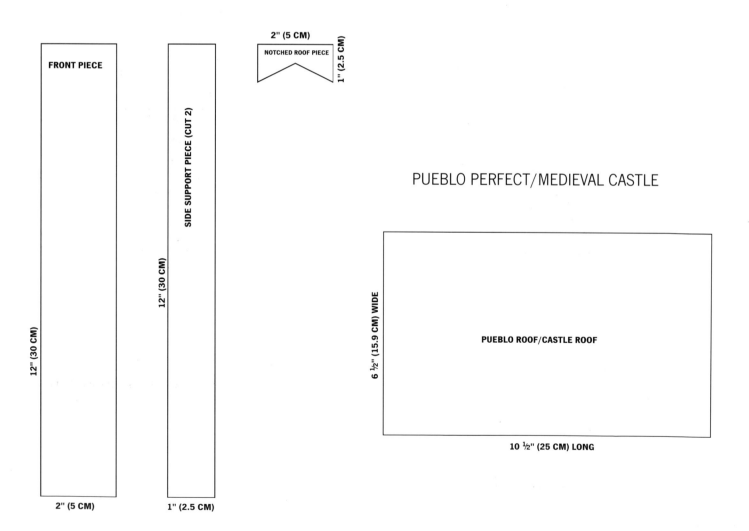

6 ½" (15.9 CM) WIDE

PUEBLO ROOF/CASTLE ROOF

10 ½" (25 CM) LONG

PORCH

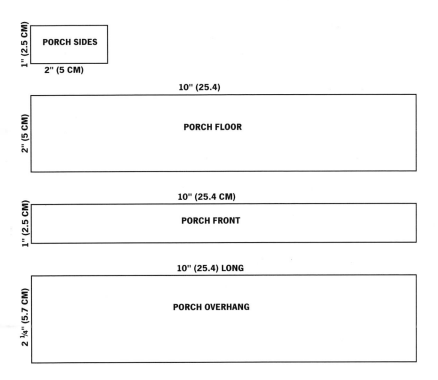

PORCH SIDES
1" (2.5 CM)
2" (5 CM)

PORCH FLOOR
10" (25.4)
2" (5 CM)

PORCH FRONT
10" (25.4 CM)
1" (2.5 CM)

PORCH OVERHANG
10" (25.4) LONG
2 ¼" (5.7 CM)

HIGH NOON SALOON
ESCAPE STAIRS

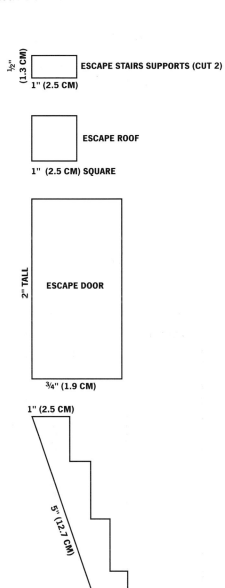

ESCAPE STAIRS SUPPORTS (CUT 2)
½" (1.3 CM)
1" (2.5 CM)

ESCAPE ROOF
1" (2.5 CM) SQUARE

ESCAPE DOOR
2" TALL
¾" (1.9 CM)

1" (2.5 CM)
5" (12.7 CM)

ESCAPE STAIRS STRINGERS (CUT 2)

DORMER

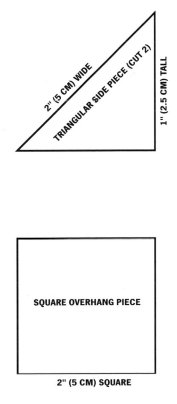

2" (5 CM) WIDE
TRIANGULAR SIDE PIECE (CUT 2)
1" (2.5 CM) TALL

SQUARE OVERHANG PIECE
2" (5 CM) SQUARE

BAMBOO-ROOFED TEAHOUSE
TEAHOUSE ROOF

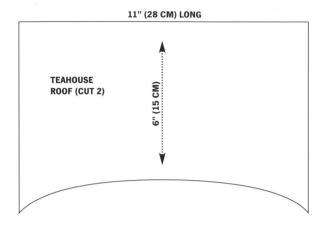

11" (28 CM) LONG

**TEAHOUSE
ROOF (CUT 2)**

6" (15 CM)

MAJESTIC MARINER'S LIGHTHOUSE

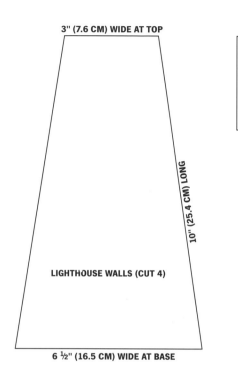

3" (7.6 CM) WIDE AT TOP

10" (25.4 CM) LONG

LIGHTHOUSE WALLS (CUT 4)

6 ½" (16.5 CM) WIDE AT BASE

LIGHTHOUSE TOP PIECE

3" (7.6 CM)

SANTA'S WORKSHOP

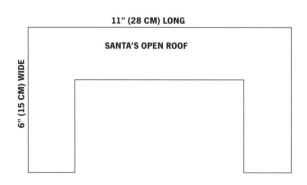

11" (28 CM) LONG

SANTA'S OPEN ROOF

6" (15 CM) WIDE

7" (17.8 CM)

SANTA'S ROOF SUPPORT (CUT 2)

**1 ½"
(3.8 CM)**

COUNTRY CHAPEL
STEEPLE BASE

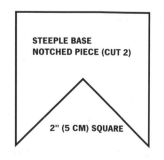

**STEEPLE BASE
SQUARE PIECE (CUT 2)**

2" (5 CM) SQUARE

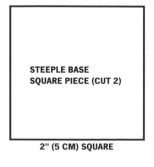

**STEEPLE BASE
NOTCHED PIECE (CUT 2)**

2" (5 CM) SQUARE

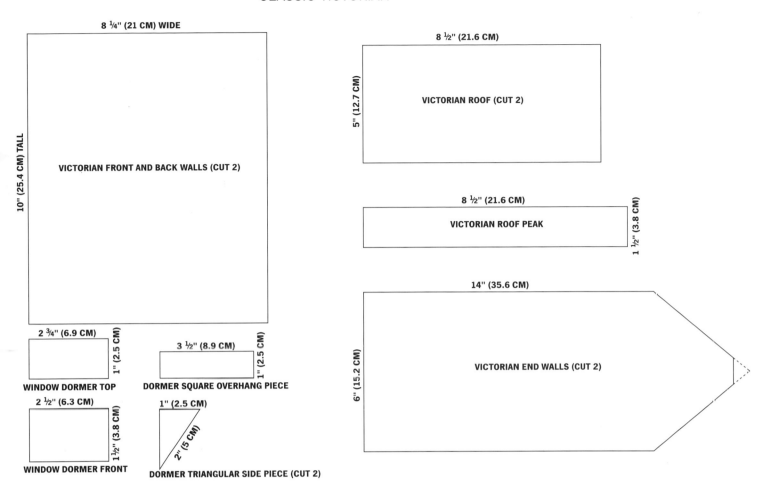

8 ¼" (21 CM) WIDE

10" (25.4 CM) TALL

VICTORIAN FRONT AND BACK WALLS (CUT 2)

8 ½" (21.6 CM)

5" (12.7 CM)

VICTORIAN ROOF (CUT 2)

8 ½" (21.6 CM)

VICTORIAN ROOF PEAK

1 ½" (3.8 CM)

14" (35.6 CM)

6" (15.2 CM)

VICTORIAN END WALLS (CUT 2)

2 ¾" (6.9 CM)

1" (2.5 CM)

WINDOW DORMER TOP

3 ½" (8.9 CM)

1" (2.5 CM)

DORMER SQUARE OVERHANG PIECE

2 ½" (6.3 CM)

1 ½" (3.8 CM)

WINDOW DORMER FRONT

1" (2.5 CM)

2" (5 CM)

DORMER TRIANGULAR SIDE PIECE (CUT 2)

Acknowledgments

Special thanks to The Grove Park Inn Resort & Spa for the assistance of its staff in preparing materials for the gingerbread houses in this book. The Inn is located in the heart of the Blue Ridge Mountains in Asheville, NC, and is home to the annual National Gingerbread House Competition each November.

Consultant

Chef Aaron Morgan is the author of *The Artful Cookie: Baking and Decorating Delectable Confections* (Lark Books, 2004), and co-author of *Making Great Gingerbread Houses* (Lark Books, 1999). Aaron has worked in the pastry arts for nearly 20 years and is currently the executive pastry chef for The Grove Park Inn Resort & Spa. His duties include conducting workshops and judging the annual National Gingerbread House Competition.

Contributing Designers

LeAnne Ash is a graduate of the Cleveland Institute of Art. She's worked as a resident artist at Odyssey Center for Ceramics Arts in Asheville, NC.

Christina Pratico Banner is a graduate of the Culinary Institute of America in Hyde Park, NY. She has made gingerbread houses competitively since 1999.

Lance B. Ethridge Sr. and his wife, Jean, enjoy baking sweet treats for their seven grandchildren. Lance works at The Grove Park Inn Resort & Spa baking rolls, breads, and lavosh.

DEC 0 8 2004

Carroll Dougall is a native and citizen of Trinidad and Tobago who works at The Grove Park Inn Resort & Spa making wedding, anniversary, and birthday cakes and desserts.

Pete and Sarah Hall are chefs at the Mountain Air Clubhouse in Western North Carolina. Their work also appears in *The Artful Cupcake: Baking & Decorating Delicious Indulgences* (Lark Books, 2004).

Todd Kindberg attends Warren Wilson College. He studies Sustainable Agriculture and Environmental Policy, and loves art, gardening, and teaching.

Diana Light has a B.F.A. in painting and printmaking, and specializes in making beautiful things from everyday objects. Contact her at dianalight@hotmail.com.

Meghan Lundy-Jones is a graduate of Warren Wilson College. She's the director of a program called The Youth Fresh Food Initiative.

Nathalie Mornu of Asheville, NC, also created projects for *Scarecrows and Lawn Figures* (Lark Books, 2004) and *Decorating Your First Apartment* (Lark Books, 2002).

Elizabeth M. Prioli was born in Edinburgh, Scotland. She's won the Grand Prize three times at The Grove Park Inn Resort & Spa annual National Gingerbread House Competition, resulting in several national television appearances.

Rose Reitzel-Perry, an award-winning pastry chef, runs Rose and Lilly's Cakes with her sister. Her work appears in *The Artful Cupcake: Baking & Decorating Delicious Indulgences* (Lark Books, 2004).

Cathy Stewart is a trained artist who's worked with metals, wood, paper, and—most recently—gingerbread. She lives in Asheville, NC.

Index

JOHNSON MEMORIAL LIBRARY
DAUPHIN COUNTY LIBRARY SYSTEM